The Lost Empire

The Lost Empire

The Story of the Jesuits
in Ethiopia
1555-1634

PHILIP CARAMAN

UNIVERSITY OF NOTRE DAME PRESS

NOTRE DAME, INDIANA

Originally published in Great Britain in 1985 by
Sidgwick & Jackson Limited

Published in the United States by the
University of Notre Dame Press
Notre Dame, Indiana 46556

Copyright © 1985 Month Publications

Maps drawn by Neil Hyslop

ISBN: 0-268-01276-8

Typeset by Tellgate Ltd, London WC1
Printed and bound in Great Britain by
Biddles Ltd, Guildford, Surrey

Contents

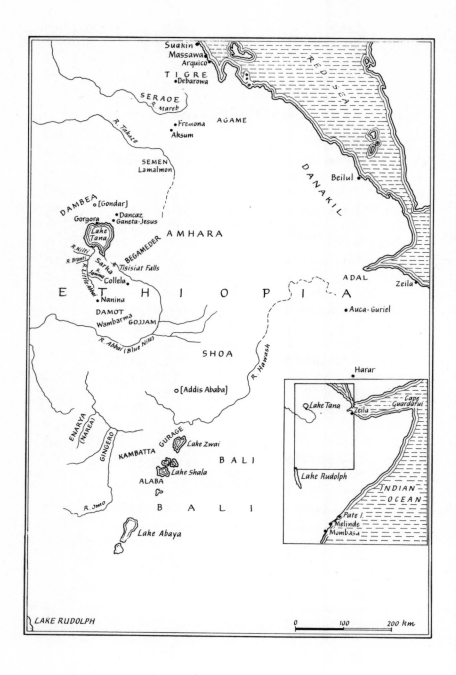

SUAKIN •
Massawa •
Arquico •

RED SEA

T I G R E
• Debarowa

SERAOE
R. Mareb

AGAME

R. Takaze

• Fremona
• Aksum

DANAKIL

SEMEN
Lamalmon

• Beilul

DAMBEA o [Gondar]
Gorgora • • Dancaz
• Ganeta-Jesus
Lake
Tana

BEGAMEDER

AMHARA

R. Kilti
R. Branti
Sarka
Jamma
R. Little Abbai
Tisisiat Falls
• Collela

ADAL
• Zeila

E   T   H   I   O   P   I   A

• Nanina

DAMOT
Wambarma GOJJAM

• Auca-Guriel

R. Abbai (Blue Nile)

SHOA

R. Hawash

o [Addis Ababa]

• Harar

ENARYA
(NAREA)

GINGERO

GURAGE
KAMBATTA
Lake Zwai

Lake Shala

ALABA

B A L I

B   A   L   I

Lake Tana
Zeila
Cape
Guardafui

Lake Rudolph

INDIAN
OCEAN

R. Omo

Lake Abaya

• Pate I.
• Melinde
• Mombasa

LAKE RUDOLPH

0   100   200 km

Introduction

Before compiling his *Dictionary*, Dr Samuel Johnson wrote a species of romance which he entitled *The History of Rasselas, Prince of Abyssinia*. His interest in that country derived from a book by a Portuguese Jesuit, Jeronimo Lobo, whose *Voyage to Abyssinia* he had rendered into English when a young man, using the text of a French translation. Lobo's book, popularly acclaimed throughout Europe, contained a first-hand, truthful and at the same time entertaining account of the 'history, antiquities, government, religion and manners' of the still mysterious kingdom of Prester John. In Johnson's romance the name Rasselas or Rassela refers to none other than Ras Cela Krestos who, like Lobo himself, plays a large part in this book. However, Lobo's *Voyage* is only a seam of the vast unexploited mine of material about Ethiopia in the period of the Jesuit mission there in the second half of the sixteenth and early seventeenth centuries.

Lobo entered Ethiopia via the small Red Sea port of Beilur in 1625 after an earlier abortive attempt to reach the country from the East African coast. Thirty-six years earlier, Pedro Paez, a Spaniard, sailing from Diu in northern India for Massawa, had been taken prisoner by the Turks off the Arabian coast and had spent seven years in captivity. He too had succeeded the second time. Both men in the course of their missionary work visited and described the springs of the Blue Nile in the Ethiopian province of Agaumeder; they were thus an acute embarrassment to James Bruce of Kinnaird, who a century and a half later in his *Travels to Discover the Source of the Nile* claimed to have been the first European to have been there. Paez's life equals Lobo's in excitement, rivals it in interest and in modern times has been compared with the adventures of T. E. Lawrence and Aubrey Herbert. Moreover his missionary achievement at least matches, if it does not surpass, that of his elder contemporary, Matteo Ricci, in China.

Although the absence of any comprehensive work on the Jesuits in Ethiopia was itself a challenge, it was almost by accident that I settled on the subject. I had first made notes for a book to contain three separate studies in Jesuit exploration: namely, the journey of Bento de Goes from Lahore through Afghanistan across the Hindu Kush and the southern Gobi desert in search of an overland route to China; the second was the repeated and eventually successful attempt, costing many lives, made by the Jesuits of Asunción to find a passage through the marshes of the upper Paraguay river to their missions in the Bolivian province of Chiquitos; then, thirdly, Paez's travels in sixteenth-century Yemen. It was this episode that led me to a more thorough study of Paez and the story of the Ethiopian mission. For this it was neccessary to sketch briefly the earlier years of the Jesuit enterprise there, which I have done in the first chapter. But the book would have been incomplete if it had ended with Paez's death, which practically coincided with his crowning achievement, the conversion of the Negus to the Roman faith. A final chapter was needed to give the events of the next ten years, which may well contain the explanation why the life of Paez has not been told before now.

Had the political situation allowed, I would have wished to have gone over the route from Massawa on the Red Sea to Fremona and on to Lake Tana, along which the Jesuits so frequently travelled. Fortunately in 1968, before I had any idea of writing this book, I spent some time in the country. Addis Ababa, Gondar and Asmara, which I visited, did not exist in Paez's day, but only Aksum, the ancient historic capital, looking then much as it did in the seventeenth century. From the air I saw Lake Tana, the mountain fortress or 'amba' Guexen, the foothills of the great plateau, and the Semen range. Thanks to these days in the country I was able to appreciate the conditions under which Paez worked there for nineteen years.

Throughout my work on this book I have been most generously assisted by Professor C. F. Beckingham, formerly Professor of Islamic Studies at the University of London and President of the Royal Asiatic Society, who has edited for the Hakluyt Society a number of Jesuit writings on Ethiopia, and who kindly read and made corrections in my typescript. I am happy also to acknowledge the help I have received from Professor Richard Pankhurst, Secretary of the Royal Asiatic Society and from my confrères, Ignatius St Lawrence, Christopher Moss and George Earle. The conclusion of the book is entirely my own, and any errors that may be detected.

P. C.

1

In 1599 Pedro Paez, a young Spanish Jesuit at Goa, reported in an excited letter to a friend in Europe news he had recently received from Agra, capital of the Mogul Empire. 'One day,' his correspondent had written, 'a Mohammedan merchant about sixty years of age was admitted to the presence of Akbar and told how he had come from Xathai by way of Mecca. Pretending to be an ambassador, he had penetrated the country and had lived in its capital, Xambalu, for thirteen years. It was a mighty empire and the king ruled over 1,500 cities, some of which had an immense population.' Many, Paez's informant had written, were followers of Jesus, but not all, for there were also many Jews and Mohammedans. Fascinated by this report, the writer, Jeronimo Xavier, a nephew of St Francis, had himself sought out the merchant, who assured him personally there was a very sizeable Christian population there and gave him details of their customs and their peculiar frocks and hats – 'like ours, only broader'.

This confirmed the accounts heard and retailed by another Jesuit, Antonio Monserrrate, of the mysterious Christian kingdom of Cathay that lay beyond the Himalayas. '*Hic dicuntur Christiani habitare*' ('Here Christians are said to be living'), he had written on his map of the region.

These men belonged to the same small but select contingent of Jesuits based at Goa, the Portuguese capital of the Indies; and their unconcealed ambition was nothing less than the conversion of the eastern empires to Rome. At this time hopes were running high all the way from India to Japan.

Akbar the Great, the Mogul Emperor of India, once more seemed to be looking favourably on Christianity. The possibility of his conversion was dazzling, for his dominions included all northern Hin-

1

dustan and stretched as far south as the central plains of Deccan. As an intellectual he was anxious to examine every system of religious belief found in his empire. He had built and adorned a splendid conference hall, still to be seen, in his palace at Fatehpur, where he presided over religious and philosophical discussions. He was a freethinker and his aim was to find an ecumenical formula that would unite the divers creeds and religious customs of his people. In this way he hoped to build a more enduring foundation for his authority. As part of this plan Akbar had invited the Jesuits to his court. 'The prince is friendly disposed towards Christians,' wrote Jeronimo Xavier, 'and towards the Señora Maria, as he calls her, and he has some fine pictures of her in his quarters. He also commends himself daily to her care and has placed two large carpets and one small one before her altar'.

In Japan expectations ran still higher. When St Francis Xavier landed at Kagoshima on 15 August 1549 he had exclaimed, 'This people is the delight of my heart.' From the very start the Jesuits had quickly adapted themselves to the ways of the country, following the conduct, manners and even the pronunciation of the upper-class Japanese; they familiarized themselves with all their niceties of ceremonial meals and, when one of their priests died, gave him all the pomp and ceremonial required for the obsequies of a shogun. In March 1585, a month before Pope Gregory XIII died in his eighty-fourth year, three Japanese princes and a party of young nobles, slim and demure in their white flowing broad-sleeved coats embroidered with birds and flowers, had received a tumultuous reception as they walked with their Jesuit catechists through the streets of Rome to a papal audience. As they knelt at his feet, the old Pope wept and said, 'Now dismiss, o Lord, thy servant in peace because my eyes have seen thy salvation.'

Five years later the Jesuits under the direction of Fr. Alessandro Valignano, a native of Chieti in the Abruzzi, who now masterminded their missions in the East, introduced a printing press into Japan; it operated first with European type but later included Japanese characters and script. At this time, when printed books were rare in parts of Europe and unknown in Japan, the Jesuits produced a Japanese translation of Aesop's *Fables* with copper-plate illustrations, religious books, catechisms, grammars and dictionaries. At Oita they had established a celebrated hospital; patients flocked there from all parts of the country, and it specialized in the treatment of leprosy and syphilis, the two afflictions most abhorrent to the Japanese. Now the Jesuits' influence was extending to agriculture, painting and the study of astronomy. It seemed only a matter of time before their religion also would be adopted by the nobles and court.

Until 1595 the Society had not penetrated the Celestial Empire of China beyond Macao and Canton. But in that year Matteo Ricci, the son of a pharmacist of Macerata in the Papal States, visited a number of provincial capitals. Still a student, he had arrived at Goa in 1578 when the Ming Emperor had effectively sealed off his empire from Europeans. The first Jesuit to enter the country had been politely asked to leave because he was uninvited; the second was told he would first have to learn the language; while the third, who stole bravely ashore from a small boat, was unceremoniously deported.

Ricci now entered the country not as a Christian missionary dressed in a tattered cassock, but in the silken robes of a Chinese mandarin, speaking the language with an almost perfect mastery. He regretted only that he could not alter the line of his nose and the slant of his eyes to adjust himself more perfectly to his hosts. Everywhere he announced himself as a 'religious who had left his native land in the distant West because of the renown of the good government of China, where he desired to remain until his death serving God, the Lord of heaven'. Had he declared his intention of preaching a new religion he would have offended Chinese pride, which would not admit there was anything to learn from foreigners. Instead he appealed to their curiosity, showing them clocks, mathematical, musical and astronomical instruments and, above all, a map of the world drawn to scale; this last was a revelation to the Chinese, on whose maps almost the entire space was filled by the fifteen provinces of China surrounded by sea and a few islands representing the countries known to them. By showing what the West had to offer in science, Ricci hoped to dispose the Chinese to give credence to the Christian faith. Wherever he went the intellectual and aristocratic élite came to visit him, but Ricci did not feel secure in the provinces until his presence had been authorized in the capital. The Goa Jesuits were right to be optimistic: on 24 January 1601 Ricci entered Peking in answer to a summons from the Emperor Wan-li. He quickly gained his goodwill, established a printing press and prepared the ground for the preaching of the gospel.

Ricci's arrival in Peking gave his brethren in Goa the incentive needed to discover whether the Cathay of Marco Polo was in fact the

China of their day. Moreover now that the Dutch were active in the Indian Ocean it was thought necessary to find an overland route to their missions in the Far East should the sea passage be cut off. The man deputed for the task was Brother Bento de Goes, a native of the Azores, an ex-soldier and the companion of Jeronimo Xavier. Experienced in caravan travel in the mountains of Kashmir, he now set out from Lahore on 6 January 1603 and crossed the Khyber Pass to Kabul; from there he made his way through eastern Turkistan to the limit of the Great Mogul's empire. Calling himself Banda Abdulla, 'servant of the Lord', with the added surname Isai or Christian, he carried letters to the Christians of Cathay and to Matteo Ricci. After crossing the Hinu Kush and the southern Gobi desert he reached the west gate of the great wall of China at Kiajuk-wan towards the end of March 1607. A few days later, on 11 April, he died at Suchow after more than three years on the trail that proved beyond doubt that China and Cathay were the same country and the Christians there a tall tale told by travellers. A lost empire had been found. In the same year that Bento de Goes left Lahore, the young Pedro Paez sailed from the northern Indian port of Diu on an equally hazardous journey. His destination was another empire that a hundred years earlier had been found but which, in the view of the Goa Jesuits, was now lost.

The search for Prester John, a powerful Christian potentate, who was thought also to be a schismatical priest, had begun in 1487. That year, John II of Portugal despatched Pero da Covilhã overland to India with orders to locate him somewhere beyond the world of Islam where he was thought to be found. This was also the fancy of the Renaissance poet Ludovico Ariosto, who made his hero fly across North Africa to land in Ethiopia at the Prester's palace, which had drawbridges made of gold, crystal columns in its halls and ceilings inlaid with pearls and precious stones. All the same, the country, wherever it was to be found, was not entirely unknown in the West. In Jerusalem pilgrims had met Ethiopian monks who had become guardians of the Holy Places on the withdrawal of the Crusaders in the thirteenth century. At the Council of Florence (1438) letters had been received from 'John, the Emperor of the Ethiopians': after the idea of crusades had been abandoned in Europe it had been taken up in all the messages of the Ethiopian Emperors to the princes of the West. On 31 August 1441 Andrew, abbot of the famous monastery of St Anthony in Egypt, had arrived

4

in Florence, to be followed four weeks later by some Ethiopian monks from Jerusalem. A commission sorted out the differences of belief and practice between the Ethiopian and Roman Churches and a Bull of Union, *Cantate Domino*, was solemnly promulgated on 4 February 1442. But nothing came of it. The religious envoys did not represent the Ethiopian Emperor, and it is even uncertain whether the Bull ever reached him. The Muslim invasions had by then made communication between Rome and Ethiopia all but impossible. When nearly a hundred years later enquiries were made, the Emperor Lebna Dengel told Pope Clement VII that a 'letter and a book' from Eugenius IV were to be found in the royal archives.

Ten years after Pero da Covilhã left Lisbon to search for Prester John, the Portuguese admiral Vasco da Gama rounded the Cape of Africa in November 1497. Putting in at Mozambique, da Gama obtained pilots to take him up the coast to Melinde. From there intermittent but unsuccessful attempts were later made by the Portuguese to reach the Prester, while da Gama, guided by an Arab pilot, crossed the Indian Ocean to Calicut on the Malabar coast, the principal emporium of the spice trade.

The absence of any strong power in the East aided the rapid establishment of the Portuguese overseas empire under Tristão da Cunha and Affonso de Albuquerque. In 1510 Goa was occupied and, in the following year, Malacca, the key to the South China Sea; Ormuz, controlling the Persian Gulf, was taken in 1515 and the sea passage up the African coast protected by fortresses at Sofala and on the island of Mozambique. However, for greater security it now became urgent to gain the goodwill of the Emperor of Ethiopia, whose vassals occupied the coast north of Melinde and the southern shores of the Red Sea.

Although the carrying trade in the East remained mainly in the hands of Arabs, there appeared now some justification for the grandiloquent title assumed in 1501 by King Manuel I of Portugal, 'Lord of the Conquest, Navigation and Commerce of Ethiopia, India, Arabia and Persia'. The Popes had also granted the Portuguese kings in their capacity of Grand Masters of the Order of Christ the right of patronage (*padroado*), which gave them virtual control of ecclesiastical appointments in a manner that made every priest and prelate overseas in some measure a servant of the crown. This concession and the failure of the Portuguese to secure the straits into the Red Sea were to have fateful consequences for the Jesuit enterprise in Ethiopia.

Although Pero da Covilhã had reached the camp of the Ethiopian Emperor he had not returned. In 1515, the year the Portuguese occupied Ormuz, the Sultan Selim I conquered Egypt and awakened the spirit of a holy war. In the same year other Muslim armies overran Yemen and moved against the highlands of Ethiopia. Their first assault was defeated by the young Emperor, Lebna Dengel, who ensnared the invaders in a gorge and totally destroyed them. 'Tranquillity and peace,' the official Ethiopian court chronicler records, 'now reigned in all the dominions of the Negus'.

Earlier, the Emperor's mother had requested military aid from Portugal; however, when in 1520 the embassy from Manuel I, led by Dom Rodrigo da Lima, reached Ethiopia the threat from Islam had passed. Six years were spent in negotiations. The Portuguese proposed to occupy Massawa to secure unimpeded entry into the country, but the Emperor was reluctant to concede this. The talks also concerned the importation of firearms which the Ethiopians lacked and urgently needed: they had already been introduced into Arabia by Muslim merchants and had accounted for the rapid conquest of Yemen. The embassy withdrew with its task unaccomplished, but its chaplain, Francisco Alvares, left a long account of the country which lifted the veil that had shrouded the realm of Prester John for nearly a thousand years.

Alvares's *True Relation of the Lands of Prester John* has special value as the only full description of the country before it was ravaged by the Muslims. He found it a prosperous empire with peripheral subject kings who acknowledged the overlordship of the Negus, to whom they paid tribute in horses, mules, damask and gold. He had much to say about the religious practices of the Ethiopians: how during Lent, which began ten days earlier than in the West, they abstained not only from meat but from cheese, butter, eggs and honey, and ate only bread and vegetables, which they took after Mass in the evening. Usually most of the monks and nuns and some of the clergy ate only every second day. Their churches were circular, with adjoining graveyards protected from the wild beasts by a high wall. Male children were baptized after forty days, females after sixty, and both received Communion after the ceremony. On Palm Sunday the women returned from church with a sprig of palm or olive in their headdress. On Good Friday the service lasted most of the day; when after the reading of the Passion a cloth was drawn from the crucifix, the people throwing themselves on the ground buffeted each other, knocked their heads against the wall, and punched themselves. This lamentation lasted for two hours. Then at the end of the service they stripped to the waist and passing out of the church were whipped by two priests standing at the doors. More revealing than his account of these religious practices was Alvares's description of the Prester himself. Lebna Dengel, then about twenty-three years old and only at the beginning of his long reign, was an elegant man of middling stature, his face round, his eyes large, his nose high in the middle. He had received the envoys seated on a dais with a crown of gold and silver on his head and a silver cross in his hand. He was dressed in a rich robe of brocade, and a fine cloth was spread over his knees down to his ankles in the manner of a bishop's apron.

In 1529, three years after the departure of the embassy, the Muslims struck again. The leader this time was the fanatical Emir Almad ibn Ibrahim, nicknamed Grañ or Left-handed, a native of Adal, the low-lying country between the port of Zeila on the Red Sea and the Ethiopian highlands. A skilful general and a born leader, he had been in the service of the Emir of Harar, now in east central Ethiopia, which already in 1520 had become the capital of a sizeable Muslim state. Grañ began his assault in 1528 and in less than a decade had overrun a great part of the country. His lightning success was due in large measure to a small highly trained body of Turks, no more than two hundred, who were proficient in the use of flintlocks. The despair of the people is reflected in the Ethiopian Chronicle, which stated that nine out of ten men renounced the Christian faith. Paez in his *History of Ethiopia* tells the story of the devastation both from the accounts of eyewitnesses and from his own observation. In 1539 the royal amba or mountain fortress of Guexen was captured with the treasures amassed there by generations of kings. Province after province fell, entire populations were massacred and stores of wealth carried off. The old monastery of Debra Libanos, the seat of Ethiopian learning, the ancient church of Aksum, where for centuries the Emperors had been crowned, and altogether more than fifty principal churches with their stores of ancient manuscripts were pillaged and burned. Lebna Dengal, refusing defeat, carried on a guerrilla warfare in the mountains.

During this time there occurred an episode far from clear in detail that was eventually to explain the Jesuit presence in Ethiopia. João Bermudes, a physician in Alvares's embassy, had stayed on at the court of Lebna Dengel. Acting as a self-appointed papal legate he appears to have agreed with the Emperor and Marcos, the Abuna (or head of the Ethiopian Church) a man over a hundred years old, on the peaceful transition of the Church's allegiance from Alexandria to Rome. In 1538 Marcos consecrated Bermudes bishop, handed over to him all his rights and prerogatives, and acknowledged his leadership of the Ethiopian Church. In Goa and in Lisbon this was interpreted as proof of the Emperor's sincere desire for reunion with Rome. His acts, however, were not ratified by Pope Paul II, who was hesitant to accept Bermudes's consecration by a schismatic bishop. But in Lisbon he was recognized as Patriarch and helped organize a military expedition under Cristovão da Gama, the son of the navigator, to aid Lebna Dengel. When da Gama, with Bermudes in his party, landed at Massawa he got news that the Emperor, an exhausted and harried fugitive, was already dead. However, on 9 July 1541 da Gama, with four hundred Portuguese, a hundred and thirty slaves and a train of guns, began his march to join forces with the new Emperor, Lebna Dengel's eighteen-year-old son, Claudius or Galawdewos, three hundred miles to the south. Everywhere he was hailed as the saviour of a Christian nation. Detachments of defeated troops joined him on the march. In Tigre, at the amba Sanet some leagues from Aksum, at the cost of eight lives, thanks to his mortars which lobbed cannon balls onto the summit, da Gama stormed a fortress that was believed impregnable. None of the fifteen hundred Moors defending it was left alive.

After dedicating the mosque as the church of Nossa Senhora da Victoria, da Gama continued south. Before he could join up with the Emperor he was attacked by Grañ's main army, which he routed twice within two weeks. The Ethiopian Chronicle for this year records how 'the children of Tubal [the Portuguese] marched up from the sea. They were bold and courageous men who thirsted after battle like wolves and after slaughter like lions.' Not long afterwards, however, da Gama was captured and taken into the presence of Grañ, at whose feet lay the heads of one hundred and seventy Portuguese slain in recent hard-fought battles. Paez later gathered details of da Gama's death. Grañ had first scourged him with his slaves' slippers, then after leading him round the camp, had twisted his beard with wax, set fire to it, pulled off his eyebrows and eyelashes with nippers, then beheaded him with his sword. Grañ's Turkish allies were outraged, for they wanted da Gama brought captive to Constantinople.

8

Claudius continued the fight with his levies and the remnants of da Gama's force. On 22 February 1543 he won a signal victory in the region of Lake Tana. Grañ was shot down by Portuguese gunners or, as some accounts have it, by a sharp shooter, and his army was routed.

On the following 10 October, at the end of the rainy season, Claudius abandoned his encampment in Gojjam and moved eastward towards the sea. On the way he came to Lalibela, where in the twelfth century, after eleven large churches had been excavated from the mountain rock by Egyptians from Cairo, the Emperor had formed them into a monastery and given it an endowment that was respected until recent times. As a shrine Lalibela was second only to Jerusalem and held out the promise of paradise. On this march Bermudes imprudently pressed Claudius to adopt Roman usages, ordering him to make a solemn submission to the Pope. The young Emperor replied in anger that Bermudes was Patriarch only of the Portuguese and called him an Arian with four gods.* But since the Portuguese troops were indispensable to him, he gave Bermudes a letter to King John III of Portugal and in a public proclamation declared the Pope the head of the universal Church. In a second letter sent by another courier and addressed to the Pope, he acknowledged Bermudes as Patriarch. But, as the Portuguese were later to learn, Bermudes had permanently alienated Claudius from Rome.

Already weakened by the Muslim invasions, Ethiopia was now threatened by the penetration of tribespeople known as the Galla. Driven west and south-west from the Horn of Africa where they were probably first settled, the Galla had already begun to attack the Ethiopian highlands earlier than the Muslims. Their pressure was continuous and was to last well into the nineteenth century. During the whole of Paez's time in the country virtually no year passed without a campaign against these fierce tribesmen. They first conquered the greater part of the Shoa province, then reaching Amhara, they settled permanently on the fringes of the Ethiopian plateau, surrounding it to the east and south.

---

* When George the Arian ousted Athanasius from the see of Alexandria in the fourth century, Arianism failed to make any progress in the young Ethiopian Church. In the province of Tigre, then the heart of the kingdom, the word 'Arian' is still a term of reprobation even among uncultivated people. Ethiopian Christians, who detest smoking, say that the first tobacco plant sprang from the intestines of Arius.

All the same Claudius, while fighting on two fronts, was able to repair much of the ravages done by the Muslims: he replaced libraries that Grañ had burnt and was said to have spent more than ten thousand ounces of gold on the purchase of manuscripts; he encouraged scribes, gave the Church most of his war spoils and himself studied the books of Scriptures with commentaries on them. His principal new church in honour of Our Lady was served by three hundred and eighteen priests, the number of the Fathers gathered at the Council of Nicaea in A.D. 325. In his own interest he was well disposed to the Portuguese remaining in Ethiopia and in return for their services gave them properties from which they were able to draw a reasonable living. It was only in succeeding reigns that the Portuguese suffered when these lands, almost always on threatened frontiers, were taken from them after they had been improved and secured, and others substituted. In Rome meanwhile Pope Paul III, who had held several Congregations in an attempt to sort out Bermudes's position, in the end had to acknowledge that it was irregular.

Against this background, St Ignatius of Loyola between the years 1546 and 1554, working with John III of Portugal and the Holy See, arranged for the appointment of a new Patriarch of Ethiopia to be consecrated with two assistant bishops and to enter the country in conjunction with a Portuguese embassy. Loyola always gave priority to the fight against Islam over all other demands on his exiguous manpower; he had first agreed to the appointment of Peter Favre, the saintly Savoyard, as Patriarch in 1546. But Favre died the same year and it was not until 1554 that João Nunes Barreto was appointed in his place with André de Oviedo and Melchoir Carneyro as assistant bishops. Ignatius had read Alvares's account of Ethiopia, and had also held frequent discussions on the country with an Ethiopian monk, Piedro, who had been in Rome since 1540: 'He has acquired,' wrote Ignatius, 'a fair fluency in Italian and also some Latin . . . and is highly regarded by the Cardinals and other prelates.'*

* In the outer sacristy of the church of the Gesù in Rome there is a painting showing St Ignatius on his knees presenting the Rules of the Society of Jesus to Pope Paul III. Behind the Pope is the Governor of Rome, on whose right is Piedro the Ethiopian. Behind Ignatius stands Cardinal Luigi Farnese, Piedro's patron.

When the appointments had been made, Ignatius drew up instructions for all Jesuits leaving Lisbon for Ethiopia and a further set of directives for the Patriarch. These documents reveal the liberal appreciation Ignatius had of the partly Jewish inheritance of an ancient Christian Church, which he insisted should be retained as far as was consistent with the substance of the Roman faith. Unessential differences such as the practice of circumcision and other Jewish customs could well be tolerated; abuses of a minor kind should not initially be challenged; changes that were needed should be introduced gradually and unacceptable customs replaced by Western festivals such as Corpus Christi processions that would appeal to the people. Portuguese settlers who knew Amharic might be used to interpret sermons, and schools were to be established for the Ethiopian youth. Then, looking beyond the religious issues, he suggested that the priests should take with them from Portugal bridge builders, construction workers, experts in agriculture as well as a physician or surgeon, in order to show the people they cared for their temporal as well as their spiritual welfare. He proposed also that they should bring with them some selected books on civil law for the improvement of governance and the administration of justice. Nothing was forgotten, not even relics of saints for the greater devotion of the people. The bishops assisting the Patriarch were to do away as much as possible with all pomp and regalia and act as pastors, taking care not to give any hint of avarice.

Both Ignatius and John III believed that, with the reputation for sanctity that had been awarded to Claudius in Europe, the appointment of a Patriarch with a small band of missionaries was enough to bring about the conversion of the country to Rome. The two assistant bishops, with twelve other Jesuits, sailed form Lisbon on 1 April 1554. One ship with three Fathers on board was lost on the flats of Pero de Banhos.

John III had ordered his Viceroy in India to send an envoy to Claudius to prepare the way for the reception of the Patriarch, who had been consecrated at Lisbon soon after the main party had sailed. Accordingly on 7 February 1555 Dr Diego Diaz, the special envoy, with two Jesuits, Gonzalo Rodrigues and a Brother, left in a convoy from Goa. Landing at Arquico they reached Claudius's camp, bringing gifts of a gold cup, a rich carpet, cushions and brocades. Rodrigues was a month at court during which he composed a treatise on the errors of the Ethiopians. Claudius was courteous, but

11

when Rodrigues asked for two monks to translate his work the Emperor made slighting remarks about it, and after reasserting for the benefit of the Jesuits a creed common in substance with the West, stated firmly what was 'my faith, and the faith of my Father, the Israelitish kings, and the faith of my flock, which is the fold of my kingdom'. Claudius continued:

> And we walk in the royal path, straight and true, and we turn aside neither to the right hand nor to the left, in the doctrine of our Fathers, the Twelve Apostles and of Paul, the fountain of wisdom, and of their seventy-two disciples, and the three hundred and eighteen orthodox men who assembled at Nicaea, and of the one hundred and fifty of Constantinople, and of the two hundred of Ephesus. Thus do I proclaim and thus do I teach, I, Claudius, King of Ethiopia, and the name of my kingdom, Asnaf-Sagad, the son of Wanad-Sagad, son of Naod.

Claudius was at pains to explain to the priests from the West that his Church adhered to certain Jewish customs, not in the manner of the Jews, but as the first Christians had done. To the Pope he wrote:

> We do not celebrate the Sabbath after the manner of the Jews . . . For the Jews do not draw water or light a fire or cook a dish of food or bake bread or go from one house to another. But we celebrate the Sabbath as the day on which we offer up the Sacrament, and we make feasts thereon even as our Fathers the Apostles commanded us in the Didascalia* . . . For on the Sabbath our Lord Jesus Christ rose from the dead, and on it the Holy Spirit descended upon the apostles in the upper room in Zion, and on it the Incarnation took place in the womb of St Mary and on it Christ will come again to reward the just and to punish sinners.

Nor did they observe circumcision as the Jews had done, but because it was the custom of the country like the scarring of the face in Ethiopia and the slitting of ears among Indians. 'What we do,' Claudius insisted, 'is not done to observe the Law of the Pentateuch, but in accordance with the custom of the people.'

Claudius's classic declaration of the faith of the Ethiopian Church was dated 23 June 1555. While waiting for an answer from the Pope

---

* A treatise purporting to have been written by the twelve apostles at the time of the Council of Jerusalem (Acts xv) but in fact a third-century composition dealing with practice more than dogma.

he had obtained an Abuna, Mark, from Cairo. Mark now excommunicated anyone at court or in the country who might be found reading Rodrigues's treatise on the errors of the Ethiopians. As Rodrigues discovered now at first hand, the Judaic observances derived from the presence of the Falashas, an indigenous people, already present in pre-Christian Ethiopia who now lived in the Semen range of mountains in southern Tigre and had certain practices in common with the Hebrews. This element explained the title 'King of Sion' in the high-sounding style of the Emperors. At the same time it marked off Ethiopian Christianity as distinct from that of Egypt which, however, provided its Church with both its Abuna and its monophysite dogma that in Christ there is only one nature as well as one person.

Meanwhile, in Lisbon, where the situation had been completely misread, an ambassador, Ferdinand de Sousa de Castello, was appointed to the court of Claudius. He sailed for Goa on 15 March 1556 along with the Patriarch Barreto. But after the Viceroy had received from Rodrigues a very different account of Claudius's attitude to the Roman Church from that current in Lisbon, he judged it unwise to allow the Patriarch and Ambassador to proceed because of the danger of an affront to Portugal. As a compromise he despatched only one of the assistant bishops, Andrew de Oviedo, with instructions to prepare the way for the full embassy.

With five other Jesuits, Oviedo landed at Arquico at the end of March 1557. Only in 1562, five years later, did any news of them reach Goa, for the Turks very shortly after their arrival had secured control of the Red Sea and had effectively sealed off the party from their base in India. Claudius again had been courteous, but had looked embarrassed on reading the letters of the Patriarch and Viceroy. However, he concealed his displeasure, showing such concern for the comfort of Oviedo that one of the Jesuits wrote: 'he was so well qualified to be Emperor, barring his obstinacy, that I am positively of the opinion there is no wiser man in the Empire.' In debates on religion at court Claudius often took the leading part and would even score points off the Bishop. According to the Chronicle, 'he defeated the Franks', as the Portuguese were called.

At the end of his patience, Oviedo left the court. In February 1559 he issued a tactless circular letter advising the Portuguese to have no dealings with the schismatic Ethiopians, whom he condemned as 'refractory and obstinate against the Church'. Fortunately for

13

Oviedo, Claudius left camp at the same time to march against the Muslims who had advanced into the province of Shoa. Later that year he was killed in battle. The Turks cut off his head, which was recovered by some merchants who took it to Antioch; there it was placed in the tomb of Claudius the martyr. A brave fighter, a generous foe, he ascribed the victories that permanently checked the Turkish advance and temporarily held back the Galla incursions to his faith, which he had so vigorously reasserted.

Since Claudius had no heirs he was succeeded by his brother Minas, a sober, conscientious ruler but violent in character. Taken in battle by Grañ in 1539, he had been held in Arabia until 1547 when he had regained his liberty in an exchange of prisoners. The Jesuits believed him perverse and cruel; 'being bred,' they wrote, 'among the Moors and Turks he had their native insolence instilled into him with their falsehood and fierceness'. Minas abrogated the liberties Claudius had allowed the Portuguese: all preaching and access to their church was forbidden; no longer could the Portuguese marry an Ethiopian or make Catholics of their wives and slaves. He took from the Portuguese their lands, kept Oviedo a prisoner for six months, then banished him from court. For another six months Oviedo and his constant Brother companion, Francisco Lopes, sheltered in a cave, living on herbs and roots, in peril of their lives from robbers and foraging soldiers, spending the day in prayer and most of the night also, for they had only the hard earth to lie on. Eventually they were allowed to settle on the threatened northern frontier on what Oviedo called a 'lonely and barren mountain', to which he gave the name of Fremona in honour of Frumentius, the apostle of Ethiopia.

In 1560 the Viceroy of India fitted out three ships with the intention of getting through to Massawa and making contact with the Portuguese, but he was turned back by the Turks. Two years later Fr. Andreas Gualdames, a native of Castile and a member of Oviedo's mission, volunteered to take to Goa news of Minas's persecution. On leaving Fremona he fell into the hands of the Turks and was killed near Massawa in August 1562. The following December the Patriarch Barreto, who had been six years in India without news from Ethiopia, died in Goa and was replaced by Oviedo who had the right of succession. Then in 1563 Minas himself died.

The long reign of Sarsa Dengel (1563-97) was taken up entirely with fighting. He drove the Moors out of Tigre and attacked

Arquico. A zealous Christian, a brave champion of lofty principles, he followed strictly all the fasts of the Church of Alexandria and sent priests to establish Christianity in the outlying province of Enarya. He tolerated the Jesuits without showing them any favours. He even gave them some hope of his conversion when, to strengthen his army against the Turks, he petitioned Portugal for workmen who could cast cannon and make gunpowder and muskets.

Settled at Fremona there was little the Jesuits could do except attend to the needs of the scattered Portuguese. News of their condition eventually reached Lisbon. The Prince Regent in the minority of King Sebastian approached Pius V to grant Oviedo permission to leave the country and close the mission. This was given on 1 February 1566. But the Patriarch replied that there were still some five or six hundred Portuguese or persons of mixed blood in the country who needed his ministrations. He pointed out also that there were many individual Ethiopians well disposed to Rome but unprepared to change their allegiance for fear of persecution; also on the frontiers were many pagan people, presumably Galla, who had sought permission from the Emperor to become Christians but had been refused because they would then have been released from slavery: the Moors bought large numbers of these pagans and sold them at a profit to the Turks; later they became Mohammedans and fought against the Christian Ethiopians.

The Patriarch lived on at Fremona in a thatched hut on a diet of teff, a cereal peculiar to the Ethiopian highlands, along with cabbage and linseed. He was deprived of almost everything. When he came to write to the Pope he had to tear off the margins of his breviary and stitch them together for lack of paper. It has been said that he undoubtedly courted martyrdom by his pugnacity. Certainly he was undiplomatic at times to the point of offensiveness and appeared to lack all the qualities that Paez was to display with such outstanding success on a similar mission. Before his death in 1577 Oviedo took the unusual step of ordaining his Brother companion, Francisco Lopes, a priest. He and Emmanuel Fernandes continued to minister to the scattered Portuguese in the frontier provinces, cut off from any contact with the world outside except for an occasional letter smuggled past the Turkish coastal guards by an enterprising merchant. In these letters the Jesuits requested the authorities in Goa either to repatriate the Portuguese community or open up communications via Massawa. Pope Gregory XIII sought to help by

15

sending a mission to the Emperor in 1585 under Giovanni Battista Britti, but it proved disastrous. One of Britti's companions was slain by pirates off Ormuz and the other was maimed, while he himself was robbed and wounded. When Fernandes died in 1583 at the age of eighty, Lopes was the only Jesuit left in Ethiopia. The decision was then taken at Goa to send Francisco Abraham de Georgiis, a Maronite Jesuit working in India, to assist Lopes. Born in Aleppo and educated in Rome, he was reckoned to have a better chance than any of reaching Fremona. But crossing to the mainland from Massawa he was discovered and martyred either on 25 or 30 March 1595. Lopes lived on another year, dying on 25 May 1596 after thirty-nine years in the country, thirteen years after the death of Fernandes. The Jesuit mission begun in 1556 with such high hopes had failed totally.

A short time before Lopes' death an Indian secular priest, Belchior da Sylva, vicar of St Anne's church, Goa, was asked by the Viceroy to make contact with the Portuguese remaining in the country. It was thought that his dark skin would enable him to pass himself off as a Muslim more easily than could a European. He was to serve as a temporary relief until a Jesuit was available. In March 1596 da Sylva sailed from Goa and travelled safely via Massawa and Debaroa to reach Fremona, where he remained until he was relieved by Pedro Paez in 1603.

2

On 22 March 1603 a Turkish ship at Diu raised anchor for Massawa, the gateway to Ethiopia, carrying Pedro Paez as a passenger in the disguise of an Armenian merchant. From that day the story of the Jesuits in that country, apart from two critical chapters, becomes chiefly the record of the young Jesuit's achievement.

The Scottish laird James Bruce of Kinnaird, who is said to have hated Jesuits as some people hate rats, was lavish in praise of Paez. After listing the priest's accomplishments, he wrote that this rare man was 'so affable, compassionate and humble that he never had the opportunity of conversing even with heretics without leaving them his friends'. He adds that Paez was 'remarkably cheerful in his temper and the most forward always in promoting innocent mirth of that species which we in England call fun'. The tribute is particularly noteworthy because in his *Travels to Discover the Sources of the Nile*, published in 1790, Bruce used every deceit to snatch for himself the glory of finding the springs of the river Nile, which had popularly been claimed for Paez.

Writing in the florid style of the Ethiopian court to the Jesuit Provincial of India at the time of Paez's death in 1622, the Emperor Susenyos compared the grief then felt in his country to that 'in Alexandria on the death of St Mark, a mourning like that in Rome on the death of St Peter and St Paul'. He concluded:

> Were this paper to be the size of the heavens and this ink the sea, we think they would not suffice to write down the fame of his goodness and the results of his labours and teaching. It is just as impossible to recount all that he did as it is to gather flowers now dead, or for today to return to yesterday and for spilt water to be gathered up.

Frequently the Emperor went to mourn at Paez's tomb and he

had a costly carpet made that in May 1626 was spread over it to remain there until it fell apart.

Pedro Paez was born in 1564 in Olmeda de la Cebolla, about eighteen miles north-west of Madrid in the administative district of Alcalá de Henares. Surrounded by hills which funnelled cold winds into the streets of the small town, it was a healthy place with a population of a few hundred who lived mainly by farming. The soil was poor but in addition to onions or *cebollas* and other root vegetables it produced crops of wheat, rye and barley. There was no feature of interest in the town apart from the parish church of St Peter. When writing to his friends in his native Castilian, Paez adds the name of Xamarillo to his signature, presumably taking it from his mother or some family relative. He had two sisters, Maria and Isabella, whom he mentions in his letters; a brother, John, the recipient of small curios, and a nephew, Gaspar; there was also a cousin, Stephen Paez, who was the Jesuit Provincial Superior first in Mexico and later in Peru.

Before entering the Society of Jesus at the age of eighteen Paez had studied at the Colegio das Artes, a constituent college of the University of Coimbra, one of the oldest in Europe, then entering the greatest period of its fame as a centre of culture. John III of Portugal, who founded the college in 1548, had entrusted it seven years later to the Jesuits, who established a regime in all major features identical with that of the Collège de St Barbe in Paris where St Ignatius Loyola had been a student. There were morning prayers and a period of class before Mass and breakfast taken in silence; classes with questions, repetitions and disputations followed the medieval method of learning in which the students were unprovided with books. The discipline was hard but the food good: a course of meat with vegetables for the main meal, except on fast days when there was smoked or salted fish. In the afternoon free time was used for public reading of the Latin poets or orators, apart from Tuesdays and Thursdays when there were games. Classes were held from three to five, then after the evening meal the *Salve Regina* was sung at nine before retirement.

As early as the fifteenth century the study of astronomy and mathematics had been introduced into Coimbra's faculty of arts and had prepared the way for the great Portuguese discoveries of Henry the Navigator, himself a very active patron of the university. Among the professors in its other three faculties, medicine, canon law and civil law, were many men of European distinction. During Paez's years there it was one of the best educational centres in the Iberian peninsula.

There is no record of where Paez entered the Society of Jesus on the completion of his course at Coimbra. But at the end of his two years' noviceship he started the usual course of philosophy at Belmonte in the province of Cuenca, about sixty miles south of Madrid. Here he made many friends among both the staff and his fellow students to whom he frequently sent messages or greetings in his letters from Ethiopia. Among others he mentions were Luís de Guzman, who volunteered like himself for the Japanese mission but remained in Spain where he was twice Provincial of Toledo; Nicholas de Almazan, from Valladolid, who was close to being elected General of the Society on the death of Acquaviva in 1615; and Ferdinand Santaren, from Huerte, who worked among the Indians in the mountains of Mexico, where he was murdered in 1616. There are many others Paez never forgot, but his closest friend at this time was Fr. Thomas Iturén, who preserved the letters Paez sent him every year; these have now become an important source for the history of seventeenth-century Ethiopia.

By comparison with Olmeda de la Cebolla, Belmonte was an important agricultural town. Its annual festival on 8 September in honour of Nuestra Señora de Gracia was celebrated with music, bonfires and bullfights. It had also a hospital or almshouse dedicated to San Andrés, where the poor were given food and lodging and taught catechism by students from the Jesuit seminary.

During Paez's years at Belmonte the Society of Jesus was entering a period of great expansion. An ever-increasing number of young men from Spain, the Spanish Netherlands, Italy, Portugal and other countries were joining the Order in the hope that one day they would be sent to work among the peoples of newly discovered countries in the remote East or West. In the last decades of the sixteenth century there was a constant flow of letters to the Jesuit Superior General in Rome begging as a favour to be sent to the Indies, Japan, China, Transylvania or to any part of the world where there was need of priests. Their petitions can be consulted today in the central Jesuit archives. These were mature men, as the sailing lists indicate, often from well-established families, whose only ambition was to live in a foreign land amidst hardship and deprivation in order to bring the gospel to people to whom it was unknown. There were others like Thomas Pounde – once a darling of the court of Elizabeth I – who, unable to communicate with Rome, gathered a group of young men inspired by the fame of Francis Xavier to follow the saint's footsteps to the Far East. Pounde himself was arrested in 1572 attempting to cross the English Channel, but his friend Thomas Stephens, an Oxford graduate, made his escape to become the first Englishman to reach India via the Cape.

Ten years later, in the short pontificate of Sixtus V (1586-90) no less than a hundred and eighty requests for the missions came from Spain alone and were filed in Rome. Enthusiasm had been quickened by accounts of the martyrdom of Rudolph Acquaviva, a nephew of the Jesuit General, and his four companions on 25 July 1583, and by the arrival in Rome in March 1585 of the Japanese princes to offer obedience to Gregory XIII. These Japanese had shown the West that, contrary to rumour, there was a harvest for the reaping in the Land of the Rising Sun. On leaving the city the following June, after saying farewell to the new Pope, Sixtus V, they had been given a reception by the various princes and cities of Spain, Italy and Portugal.

During his studies at Belmonte Paez took his first step towards Ethiopia. His request to Acquaviva to be sent abroad is dated 8 May 1587. In his petition he spoke of the yearning he had for the missions from the time he was a novice, so great that he felt compelled to write to Rome. 'I had hoped and asked our Lord that your Reverence would send me to China or Japan without my asking,' he wrote:

> But now it seems that I would not be corresponding to what I have been given to understand, if I did not ask your Reverence to send me to one of these missions. I mention these countries because of the great inclination I have towards them, but at the same time I would find it most acceptable to go to any other place to which your Reverence might wish to send me, in spite of the fact that I feel I lack the gifts demanded for such undertakings.

These phrases he uses are not very different from those found in other petitions. In his opening sentence Paez reveals that before joining the Society he was 'very far away' from the life he was now leading; and in concluding he hints that he had then been no model of all the religious virtues. 'So for the love of the Lord,' he writes, 'I beg your Reverence to send me to that place where I can give my life for him who has saved it from so many dangers and storms that beset it in the world.'

While most letters of this kind received a reply of paternal encouragement with an exhortation to prepare for the labours of the missions by diligent study, Paez's request was immediately effective. Before finishing his course of philosophy he was on his way to Lisbon in March 1588 on the first stage of his journey to Goa.

From Lisbon, now rebuilt after the earthquake that had destroyed over fifteen hundred houses in 1531, the fleet for India left regularly at the end of March or in early April to catch the trade winds. Through the city markets Paez would have seen most of the treasures of the East enter Europe, along with some of the ten or twelve thousand slaves from Guinea and West Africa sold there every year and reshipped to the South American plantations. The Jesuits sailing for India in 1588 embarked on 6 April; six of them, including Paez, on the *São Thomé*, and another four on the flagship *São Cristovão*. On the foremast of each ship of the flotilla fluttered the red cross of the Order of Christ, which also decorated the sails.

An Indian ship of 550 tons, carrying up to three hundred and sixty passengers and a crew of over a hundred, had to take on water, wine, salted meat, hundredweights of sardines, live chickens, mortars, spare anchors and spare sails sufficient until supplies could be renewed four or five months later at Mozambique. On the first days out decks were piled high with boxes and barrels of provisions which were later stored below. In the most favourable conditions the voyage lasted six months but it could take almost twice as long if the fleet was forced to winter in Mozambique. Making first for the Cape Verde Islands, it sailed down the coast of Guinea; then, some seven or eight degrees north of the Equator, it would run into the Doldrums – a sea without winds where it might lie becalmed for forty or sixty days in unbearable heat: food spoilt, drinking water turned yellow, wine tasted like vinegar, salted meat began to rot and the hold became like a steaming oven. The trade winds, rising suddenly, would then fill the sails and the fleet would ride across the Equator towards the Brazilian coast at Cabo Santo Agostinho, then south-west again down the coast keeping some seventy or one hundred leagues out to sea for fear the currents might take it back towards Portugal. At this point on the far side of the Abrolhos reef it met the north-west trade winds that carried it back across the Atlantic to the region of Tristão da Cunha and on round the stormy

Cape to Mozambique. From there in the autumn monsoons the fleet would take about thirty-five days via Melinde to reach Goa.

Paez was fortunate not to have been assigned to the flagship. Among the four Jesuits who sailed in it was Sebastian de Morais, the first bishop destined for Japan. The question of establishing a bishopric there had been under discussion since 1564 but it was only shortly before the spring fleet of 1588 sailed from Lisbon that de Morais had been consecrated. He was never to reach his see. While the *São Cristovão* was lying becalmed off the coast of Guinea an epidemic broke out on board. The Bishop, who had been nursing the stricken passengers in spite of the captain's protests, fell sick and on 19 August died within sight of Mozambique, where he was buried in the church attached to the fortress. Three days later, Antonio Rodrigues, a young priest of thirty-four, died of the same epidemic; thirty leagues out, less than a fortnight later, on 4 September the student Antonio Luís fell a victim and was buried at sea. The only Jesuit survivor was Brother Gaspar de Castro; he had been infirmarian at the house in Coimbra. As if to make up for the losses, de Castro was later ordained and sent to Japan. On his arrival at Goa he wrote a moving account of his experience on the flagship to Claudio Acquaviva, the Jesuit General.

The *São Thomé* docked safely at Goa in September 1588. With Paez there were two Portuguese Jesuits on board, two Italians and another Spaniard. It was only some time later that they learned the fate of their brethren in the *São Cristovão*, but for the present nothing could spoil their excitement when they stepped ashore at the great city where East and West met at every crossing. Lying four miles up the Mondovi river on the north-eastern part of the island of the same name, and enclosed within walls that had been raised in height after its capture, Goa was further protected by a moat on the landward side. The high roof of the cathedral, built on the site of the demolished mosque, and the twin spires of the Franciscan church, towered over the whitewashed dwellings. The river was always alive with ships of different nations and in the Rua Direita, the main artery of the city, Hindus, Muslims, and merchants from Armenia and Indonesia met Portuguese who traded in ginger, spices and pepper. Passing the streets to the Jesuit house, Paez would have met Arab horse dealers, slaves from the African coast, Hindu merchants from Cambay with their pointed upturned shoes, farmers from the countryside, Syrians and Chinese. For a Jesuit, however, Goa was the shrine of Francis Xavier, who had set out from here for the Far East. Xavier's body, buried in lime after his death on the island of Sancian off the Chinese coast in December 1552, had been brought back here incorrupt and placed in the church of the Society of Jesus.

At the Jesuit College of St Paul, a short distance from the city centre, some forty young men werre preparing for the priesthood when Paez joined the community to begin his course of theology. On Sundays and feastdays they would interrupt their studies to teach catechism in the city churches, visit the prison or organize the group baptisms that were held with great solemnity. On Thursdays they would take walks through the island villages with their groves of coconut and fields of rice and millet, passing the huts of Hindus with their banana plants, wide-spreading mango and jack-fruit trees.

Paez had been barely three months in India when the Provincial of Goa, Pedro Martins, *asked him whether he was prepared to accompany Antonio Monserrate to Ethiopia. Monserrate, a Jesuit, had returned four years earlier from the court of the Mogul Emperor Akbar at Agra. In a letter to his friend Thomas Iturén at Belmonte dated 16 February 1589, Paez explained how he came to be chosen:

> Two days before the feast of the Conversion of St Paul [25 January], the Provincial . . . asked to see me. He told me that a mission of great importance was in preparation and that, after hearing the opinion of some senior Fathers, he had decided that I should go as companion to Fr. Antonio Monserrate, who had been charged with it. But since the enterprise involved great physical hardship and numerous risks he insisted that I should tell him if I had any reason for refusing it.

Martins knew what he was asking. As preacher to Sebastian of Portugal, he had accompanied the King on his African expedition in 1578 and had been taken captive by the Moors. Then in 1586 on his way to India he had been shipwrecked on the reefs of Judia off the coast of Mozambique and attacked by savages. When in 1592 he ceased to be Provincial he was consecrated at Goa Bishop for Japan

---

* For the purposes of administration the Jesuit Order was divided into units called provinces, determined normally by geographical or national factors, under a Superior known as the Provincial, who was responsible to the Superior General in Rome.

to replace Sebastian de Morais. Now he did not have to wait for the acceptance of Paez, who told him at once that he had volunteered for the Indies in the hope of just such an assignment. The Provincial replied that he had received precisely the answer he had expected.

Unlike Paez, Antonio Monserrate could in some respects be said to have been an obvious choice. A Catalan born in Vic de Ozona in 1536, he had won a reputation as a diplomat at Agra at the court of Akbar the Great, who ten years earlier had entrusted him with the post of tutor to his second son, Prince Murad. When in 1580 Akbar's brother had rebelled in Kabul, Monserrate had been asked to accompany the Emperor's army on a punitive expedition, but at Jalalabad in east Afghanistan on the Kabul river he had fallen sick and could go no further. In 1582 he had joined Akbar's embassy to the Viceroy at Goa, where at the request of the Jesuit General, Claudio Acquaviva, he had made an abstract of the diary he had dept at the imperial court. In it he describes the appearance, character and clothing of the Mogul Emperor, his palaces, guards, officials, elephants, revenues and cities, his amusements, including polo, the constitution and practices of the army, and his own adventures at the hands of fanatics in the Khyber Pass.

Paez, however, had been singled out from the young men who had sailed with him from Lisbon, from students senior to himself at Goa and from the more seasoned priests who staffed the Jesuit establishments in India. It was an exceptional appointment by any standard of procedure among the Jesuits. Monserrate, writing to Acquaviva two weeks after sailing, speaks of Paez's youth, then quotes the Book of Wisdom, 'Understanding, this is man's grey hairs, Untarnished life, this is man's old age.' He adds that Paez was chosen because he was a student of great promise and was prepared to endure anything. But his charm must already have been evident: Fr. Emmanuel d'Almeida, writing about him in his *History of Ethiopia*,* says that he was 'so affable in manner that he captivated the hearts of all who had any dealings with him'. Unfortunately there is no portrait of him as there is of other missionaries, but it would seem that he had also striking presence, for Almeida adds that he was a tall man with a florid complexion and lively mind who conquered all by making himself the servant and slave of all.

* Sections of Almeida book, printed in full by Beccari, are included in Beckingham and Huntingford, *Some Records*.

This fresh mission to Ethiopia was being undertaken on the initiative of Philip II of Spain, who as Philip I of Portugal, after the union of the two crowns in 1580, was the supreme patron of missionary activity in the East. He was constantly giving detailed instruction to his Viceroy concerning the building of churches, the financing of colleges and the disposition of priests. Philip had never lost interest in Ethiopia, for he was anxious to bring the Emperor into union with the Roman church and have him as an ally against the Turks. More than once he had urged the Viceroys to study ways of gaining entry into the country, whether through Melinde on the East African coast, or through Alexandria or some other harbour, and to look into measures for a possible military occupation of Massawa. The Turkish mastery of the Red Sea was now well established, and it was only through the occasional smuggled letter that any contact was maintained with the Portuguese still in the country.

Philip II ruled that the Jesuit mission, reduced then to one priest, Francisco Lopes, was to be kept open and re-enforced with new men. On receiving the King's instructions Dom Duarte de Menese, the Viceroy of India, had approached the Jesuit Provincial of Goa and insisted on the immediate despatch to two Fathers to Ethiopia. As no priest companion for Monserrate was available, it was decided to ordain Paez. 'The Viceroy persuaded the Archbishop of Goa,' Paez continues, 'to proceed at once, and so it happened that on the feast of the Conversion of St Paul [25 January] I was ordained subdeacon, then deacon the following Friday and finally priest on the Sunday.'

Early in February 1589 the two priests set sail. On the second day out contrary winds forced them to put in at Elephanta, a small island in Bombay harbour, six miles east of the present city, so named by the Portuguese from a large stone elephant that stood near the old landing place on the south side of the island. It was famous for its temple caves carved out of solid rock about the year A.D. 800. Here on a high hill Paez visited a temple in which there were forty tall and finely cut columns and around it numerous chapels full of delicately chiselled figures of Hindu deities. The principal idol had three heads, he told Iturén, but the entire site was deserted except for bats, which looked as large as pigeons. Alongside two of these idols lay some food, which mice were busy eating. These were the Brahminic rock temples, the most important of which, the Great Cave, was supported by six rows of columns, with six columns in each row.

25

Paez had seen the most striking of the sculptures, the famous three-faced bust, which stood at the back of the cave facing the entrance. It was a representation of Siva in his threefold character of creator, preserver and destroyer. It was seventeen feet ten inches in height and a line drawn round the three heads at eye level measured twenty-two feet nine inches. 'I had chanced on this site,' Paez wrote, 'but I was told that not far away was another still finer temple which they call the pagoda of Canari.' His informant could only have been referring to the caves of Kanheri in a wild and picturesque valley on the island of Salsette, which since their discovery in 1534 had been an object of great wonder to the Portuguese. Paez was unable to see them for the party re-embarked the same evening.

Without further incident they reached Bassein, twenty-five miles north of Bombay, where the Jesuits deployed their largest number of men after Goa and Cochin. With the taxes levied on the numerous villages in the district and with other imposts the city was a rich source of revenue for the Portuguese in India. Here on the Sunday before Ash Wednesday Paez celebrated his first Mass in the chapel of the Jesuit College. While waiting to embark on the next stage of his journey he started to learn Persian, the lingua franca of northern India and widely used in the western Indian Ocean. This was a sensible measure, for he and Monserrate, who could already speak the language, proposed to sail in a Turkish ship as far as Mocha on the Gulf of Aden, passing themselves off as Armenian merchants, and from there through the Straits of Aden as far as Massawa; then crossing to Arquico on the mainland they could follow the route to Fremona, Lopes's base in Ethiopia.

That was their plan. However, the Viceroy, who had been made responsible for their reaching Ethiopia, had contacted a wealthy Portuguese merchant in Bassein, Aloysius de Mendoço, who traded with the Red Sea ports. The merchant had undertaken to get the priests a passage from Diu directly to Massawa in one of his chartered ships. Thus at the end of February the Jesuits set out in a rowing boat across the bay from Bassein to Diu and ran into a storm that lasted all through the night. Everyone in the boat, believing they were lost, covered their heads with their cloaks so as not to see the others perish. But it was calm again at sunrise and that night they entered Diu disguised as Moors. All the time they were here Monserrate did not venture into the town for fear of being recognized, for he had been well known in Goa during the last four or five years

26

since his return from Agra. Paez was therefore left to negotiate the next stage of their journey; whenever he appeared in the streets the Portuguese children, taking him for a Moor, threw stones and mud at him. On one occasion, on entering the Portuguese fortress, he was assaulted by a guard who was about to run him through with his sword when he was held back by another soldier who recognized him.

Certainly Diu offered them the best chance of a ship to Massawa, for the city contained a number of important markets, famous especially for their cotton goods, and was the home also of Hindu merchants whose ships were to be found in all the seas between Suez and Malacca. Here in 1538 the Portuguese garrison of the newly built fortress had halted the advance of the Turks in their drive to evict them from India.

The Fathers were disappointed, however. No ship's captain was prepared to risk sailing with them on board. Despairing of finding any other way of reaching Ethiopia, the priests accepted the offer of an Armenian to take them up the Persian Gulf to Basra and from there overland to Aleppo. This was the old route that the Venetians had taken to bring the spices of the East to Europe; it was less used now that the trade was in the hands of the Portuguese, who by sailing round the Cape were able to avoid the taxes levied on Eastern merchandise by the Islamic rulers along the ancient trail. From Aleppo they planned to take the road south to Cairo and from there travel by caravan and sea to Massawa.

With this intention the Jesuits embarked at Diu on 5 April. At Muscat, then 'a very small village full of Muslims' but in Portuguese hands since 1508, they put in for water. There they met a Moor who was making ready to sail for Zeila in northern Somalia. When he offered to take them on board it seemed that he had been sent them by providence. While the ship's captain was making preparations for the voyage, the Fathers stayed at Ormuz, at the entrance to the Persian Gulf, a fortress town set against the desert sands where merchants from Persia, Arabia, Turkey and Armenia came to trade in horses and other goods. The Fathers lodged with the Augustinian friars in their very poor monastery. While there Paez contracted a fever and seemed unlikely to make a quick recovery. The Moor, not to lose the trade winds, insisted on sailing. After conferring with the Portuguese Governor of the fortress, Monserrate decided to go on alone, but, just as he was about to raise anchor, word came that eight pirate vessels were lying out to sea to board his ships. There was a further delay while the Governor swept the seas clear. Paez recovered in the interval and embarked with Monserrate on the night of Christmas 1589. It was almost eleven months since they had left Goa.

For the first few days all went well. On New Year's Day 1590 they ran into a storm that damaged the ship's rudder. The Moor was forced to find shelter at one of the islands of the Kuria Muria archipelago off the south Arabian coast. The first European to describe them, Paez says that the people there were poor and miserable, and covered their houses with weeds washed up on shore. They lived on fish, which they dried in the wind and ate raw. As there was no wood on the island for the repair of the rudder, the Moorish captain was compelled to rig out a small boat which he hired to continue on his way to Zeila. While he was engaged on this the crew of his own ship, in violation of their agreement with him, had gone off on a transport to the mainland where they spread news of their imminent departure.

After seven or eight days the Moor set sail. The winds were against him and he was driven towards the coast, where he was observed. Immediately two small pirate ships put out to sea, boarded his vessel and took it as a prize to Dhofar, then a small town on the coast of Shihr. Like Ormuz, Dhofar traded mainly in incense, a humid port with a beautiful shoreline and a poverty-stricken population. On landing the priests were stripped naked and put in prison for five days; there was a famine in the town and they were given little to eat. What was worse, it was assumed, not without some ground, that they were spies on their way to Ethiopia to persuade the Emperor to make war on the Turks. Finally it was decided that they should be sent to the 'king of that region', the designation they gave to the ruler of Hadhramaut.

On the first stage of their journey they were taken in a small boat down the coast to avoid passing through the territory of the ruler of Qishn, the chief town of the Mahra sultanate in east Hadhramaut. Disembarking at the mouth of a wadi, which Paez assumed to be the dried-up bed of a large river, they were taken inland across a rough trackless terrain. On the first day they covered eleven miles, stopping the night at a village where Paez was given some ill-fitting Moorish shoes. The following day his feet became so swollen and blistered that he cast the shoes off and continued barefoot. Monser-

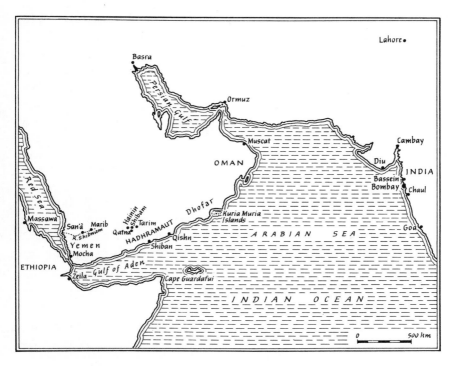

Map indicating the places through which Pedro Paez passed in his first abortive attempt to reach Ethiopia, February 1589 to November 1596

rate, older and weaker, was unable to keep pace with the camels and on the third day was permitted to sit on top of the baggage they carried. When the party stopped to feed their animals the priests gathered locusts which they grilled and ate. 'We could not manage such nauseous food,' wrote Paez, 'so they gave each of us a cake baked in ashes and made from the flour we had taken on board with us; but the cakes were so small that we were always hungry.' There was a day when passing through a long valley they seemed to see ahead of them a large river and became excited at the prospect of at last drinking some fresh water, but the sight proved a mirage. 'When we got there,' Paez recorded, 'we saw it was only sand that had been whipped up by the wind and was moving like water, never rising more than three or four palms above the ground.' Almost blinded by the desert sun, they continued their journey, keeping a fast hold on a piece of linen cloth that they held on their heads for protection against sunstroke.

After six days during which they did not meet a living person they reached Tarim, 'a large city in Arabia where the people had never before set eyes on a Christian'. News of their arrival spread and crowds gathered to gaze at them as they were taken through the city gates:

> At first they stared at us without saying a word; then they asked our escort whether we believed in Mohammed. On getting the answer 'no', they began calling us Cafaráns, the Arabic for outlaws, adding a number of other gibes and insults. They spat in our faces and punched us with their fists. There was nothing our guards could do, there were so many people in the streets that not even the camels could make headway. We were then hurried off to shelter in a house, for the boys were now picking up stones to hurl at us.

To avoid further street scenes the priests were put on the road early next morning.

That is all Paez wrote about Tarim in the wadi Hadhramaut lying to the east of Shiban. He could have seen nothing of its mosques, said now to number three hundred and sixty, for it was a fanatically Muslim town where even today women come out into the street to stare at Christians.

For fourteen more days, ill-shod and clothed only in cotton vests, Paez and Monserrate walked on in extreme heat. Paez tells how they now made their way westward into the hills and the cultivated district of Hadhramaut:

30

The first day and the two following we passed numerous towns, but in none did we have the same experience as at Tarim. In the hills there were many ruins of fortresses, and our guards told us that they had been constructed by Christians in an earlier epoch. In the last of these towns lived the brother of the King [of Hadhramaut], called Zafar. This prince gave orders that we should be brought into his house, which was a large building. He was seated on carpets dressed like a Moor and received us with courteous words, begged us to be seated and gave us chacuâ, which is a drink made with water poured on to a fruit which they call *bun*: the people of the country drink it very hot in place of wine.

In this letter to Iturén, Paez is not only the first traveller from the West to describe Hadhramaut, which remained unknown to Europeans until the nineteenth century; he is also one of the first to mention coffee, which was not introduced into Europe until later. The Arabic word he uses here, *chacuâ*, passed into French military jargon as *dakuâ* when Algeria was conquered in 1830. His description of the country is borne out by aerial photographs taken in the early 1930s that reveal the ruins of a large number of fortresses. The 'last of these towns', as Paez calls it, where the King's brother lived, would have been Qatna, at the strategic point where two wadis from the south converge on the wadi Hadhramaut.

On leaving, the Fathers walked through the night until they reached Hainin, two hundred and seven miles north-east of Aden. Here the Sultan Omar resided. First, the Jesuits were taken to the fort, a lofty building of clay, and put into a sentinel's box on the wall, where they endured more trouble from sightseeers. Two days later the sultan ordered them into his presence. Acting as interpreter at the audience was a Burmese woman who had been captured with eight Portuguese in the time of Omar's father; the Portuguese had died in captivity but she had become a Muslim. Clad in a fine green robe the sultan sat on a dais covered with a rich brocade. On his head he wore a turban embroidered with gold. Paez considered his person 'comely' and judged that he was about forty years old.

The sultan asked the captives politely who they were, where they had started their journey and why they were making for Ethiopia. On their giving satisfactory answers he ordered that they should be given back their breviaries, books and papers, which had been taken from them when they were first captured, and he told his servants to provide them with all the food they needed. Although during the four complete months they stayed at Hainin the priests had nothing to eat but black bread and water, Paez is careful to point out that they suffered only the same privations as other prisoners, for, as he says, 'this province of Arabia which they call Hadhramaut is very poor. The largest part of it is desert and there is extremely little cultivation because the rains are so rare.'

Food apart, their treatment at Hainin was liberal. During these months Fr. Monserrate put the finishing touches to a work he had left incomplete on his departure from Goa. Entitled *Mongolicae Legationis Commentarius*, it was a connected narrative, based on the diary he had kept during his embassy to Akbar's court. He wrote:

> I had no time or opportunity to return to my task, until I was captured by my enemies, the Musulmans, near Dhofar in Arabia . . . The Musulman king of Omar allowed my slender baggage and books to be returned to me. He also permitted me a considerable degree of freedom, though I was still held in custody. For I was granted four months of leisure, in which I was able to make the necessary corrections and additions to what I had written. For by the singular goodness of God I had then to bear none of the bitterness of captivity except for the mere fact of being a prisoner. My chief solace was the companionship of Father Peter Paez (to whom I made my confession), and next to this I found comfort from holy books and from our morning and evening prayers.

While they were at Hainin the priests were even given some prospect of release. First they were told that the sultan was anxious to free them, but later that he felt obliged by the terms of his vassalage to pass on any 'Portuguese' prisoners to his overlord, the Turkish Pasha of San'â in Yemen. Paez's statement to this effect is proof that at this time the representative in Yemen of the sultan at Constantinople exercised real authority in the country – a surprising situation, for the Turkish domination of Yemen that began in 1517 was marked by an almost continuous series of revolts. Only in 1569 was Hassan Pasha, to whom Paez was now despatched, able to get rid of the last indigenous prince of the Yemenite Mutahride dynasty, who had waged a long and merciless war against the Turks. Hassan Pasha was to govern Yemen until 1604, but from 1597 he was again troubled by rebellions. Paez's years in Yemen therefore fell within the short period of Hassan Pasha's uncontested rule. Ten years earlier or later all the caravan routes would have been cut, with the country in a state of insurrection.

32

It was four months before Paez and Monserrate were on the road again. The journey to San'â proved 'very hard', although the sultan provided them with camels and sent with them four horses as a gift to the pasha in order to safeguard himself against his extortionate demands. He also gave instructions that the priests should lack nothing because, as he said, they asked nothing for themselves.

Paez's description of the country through which they now passed is the earliest known account of the interior of Yemen by a European; until well into the twentieth century the two Jesuits were the only Europeans to reach San'â from Hadhramaut.

On the first stage of their journey they were taken to a fort which was the last outpost of the sultan's domain. There the camels were watered. Then for four days and nights they crossed a totally arid desert. They steered by the sun and the stars and, fearing both might later be concealed by clouds, they rode through the entire day and night. They were anxious also to escape robbers lurking in the desert. On the fifth day they reached a well and rested. Then going up into the hills they came to a 'small place called Melquis', where Paez saw the 'ruins of some very large buildings and stones with ancient inscriptions which the natives of the country could not read'. He was told that it had once been a great city and that the Queen of Sheba used to graze large herds there – a remark which made him reflect that, if this were true, then her dominions embraced both Ethiopia and parts of Arabia.

Nobody from the West before Paez had seen this ancient city of Marib with its vast ruins and Himyaritic inscriptions. Today it is no more than a small, almost deserted village, but in ancient times it is depicted as a land rich in perfumes, incense and gold. Lying forty miles inland at an altitude of nearly four thousand feet, it might well have been the capital of the Queen of Sheba. The next European to report on the site was the French archaeologist J. Halévy; in 1870, he gave the first scientific description of the ruins, which include a dam built in the sixth century B.C., one of the great engineering feats of antiquity. The dam collapsed in the sixth century A.D. flooding the countryside, which explains why Paez found only 'very ancient ruins of towns and fortresses jutting out from the desert sands'. For six centuries at least this had been a centre of the civilized world. The tradition, first recorded by Paez, that it was the Queen from Marib who visited Solomon has the support of present-day archaeologists.

From Marib, continuing across the mountains, they took another twelve days to reach San'â. Paez was struck by the poor lives of the people and the unsuitability of the name 'Arabia Felix', which he supposed the ancients gave it by 'rule of contraries or else in error'. Most of the land was left uncultivated, the crops he saw were very poor, and consequently the natives suffered from hunger. Their staple food was millet, though some wheat, barley and dates were also grown. They had a tawny complexion, and dressed poorly; the women grew their hair long, curled it with irons and then greased it with butter. Paez had already noticed at Hainin how, when mourning for the death of one of Omar's daughters, the women would put dust on their hair and then gathering on the flat roof of their houses would form two lines, beat their breasts, lament loudly and embrace each other.

On this part of their journey they crossed a 'large river', which would have been a seasonal torrent. During the crossing Monserrate, weary before the start, fell from his camel. As the water was shallow, he struck his head on the rocky bed and became unconscious for a long time.

Finally they left the hills behind and came out on to the stony plateau on which San'â, the capital of Yemen, stood, seven and half thousand feet above the sea and one of the most picturesque cities of Arabia. Paez was impressed by this 'great city with its strong walls and mighty bulwarks of earth', but he said that it had declined rapidly after it had been captured by the Turks. He was told that San'â had its origins in pre-Islamic times and in the sixth century had been under Ethiopian control. He reckoned that when he was there the city contained about two and a half thousand houses, five hundred of which belonged to Jews, who had their own quarter and were free to practise their religion.

At the entrance to the city the Fathers were received by the Subashi or police chief with a large escort of foot soldiers and some cavalry. Ordering the kettledrums to be beaten he made the priests walk in front of his mount as if in a triumph. They passed through the city gate where until recently the heads of executed criminals had been displayed, and he conducted them to the fortress, which was also the pasha's palace. There they were questioned by the steward of the palace, who presumed that they were spies and put them in prison. Twenty-five Portuguese and five Indians were also prisoners – all at such odds among themselves that they were ready to murder

34

each other; they had been taken captive off Melinde on the African coast. Cast together here the climate added to their ill temper, for it was a humid and unhealthy city with a high rate of mortality from jaundice, malaria and dysentery. At first Paez was put in chains but Monserrate, in consideration of his age, was given the liberty of the prison.

San'â was full of gardens and orchards producing, as Paez wrote, 'almost all the different kinds of fruit we have in Europe'. The pasha, at one time a gardener to the Great Turk himself, employed the prisoners in his own garden after the priests had been incarcerated for about a year. Later he gave them their own prison room, which was large enough to partition off part of it as a chapel. 'He was an Albanian by race,' says Monserrate; 'an Albanian is commonly called an Arnautes by the Turks, and an Allanesian by the Portuguese, both names being derived from the name of the principal town of the tribe, Alessio.'

The Jesuits remained in San'â for almost three years. Paez used the time to study Hebrew, Persian and Arabic. From here he was able to write to his friend, Thomas Iturén, at Belmonte:

> We have an oratory with one well set up altar, at which Christians come to pray to God before they go out to work in the morning and again on their return in the evening. For our comfort we try to celebrate the feasts of the Church as best we can, emulating the observances of Christian countries.

At dusk Vespers and Compline were sung, and before dawn a 'dry'* Mass was said or sung to the accompaniment of a guitar that one of the captives had been able to keep. At the offertory the bread was blessed, and at the elevation a crucifix was raised for the congregation to honour. For greater devotion the captives went frequently to confession, and in Holy Week they carried out the ceremonies with as much solemnity as possible, displaying once again the crucifix in place of the Sacrament.

In his letter dated 17 July 1593 Paez describes the behaviour of the people when on 30 May 1593 a total eclipse of the sun occurred at San'â. He writes:

> The sun was obscured for a good time during which there was wailing

---

* Unable to obtain wine, the priests could only recite the words of the Mass omitting the consecration prayer.

all over the city. Many asked what this signified. They marvelled to see such a phenomenon. The leading men of the place said in that hour two kings were dying but they did not know where. The following day the soothsayers and diviners gathered in the house of the pasha to cast dice in order to find out the meaning of the eclipse.

At the time of writing Paez was depressed. His captors, he told Iturén, 'hold with an unshakable faith that every event in a man's life is determined by fate and is written on his brow, so that nothing can possibly prevent it happening'. He feared the dice that dictated the death of the two kings might also reveal that he was to remain in prison for the rest of his life: 'All they do is determined by the throw of dice and by divination. If the dice decide it is not opportune to set us free, they will never do it. But may Our Lord be served. It will be no small mercy if simply and only for love of him we end our days in captivity.'

Five days after Paez wrote this, Monserrate sent a petition to Fr. Acqaviva. He told the General that although the Provincial of India had tried and was still trying to get them released he had achieved nothing. The reason for his failure was that negotiations had to be conducted through either Moors or heathens. The Moors would not set them free for fear of Mohammed, and the pagans, though they were sympathetic, dared not do anything to help. He suggested that one of the consuls in Constantinople might be approached, or one of the Jesuits if there were any still there. Monserrate believed that only a direct petition to the Great Turk would bring their captivity to an end. In the margin of the letter, now in the Jesuit archives in Rome, Acquaviva's secretary wrote the words, 'Written to Venice'.

Monserrate now helped Paez in his study of languages. He also made another revision of his *Commentarius*. 'After four months of leisure [at Hainin],' he wrote, 'I once more had to lay aside my literary tools, for I was ordered to proceed to San'â where a Turkish Viceroy resides. . . . He ordered my books to be restored to me, whereupon I returned to my task and yet further revised, corrected and added to my records, and freed them from blemishes.'

He also wrote two other books in captivity: the first, an account of his departure for Ethiopia; the second, a natural history of Arabia. These last two books have been lost, but surprisingly the *Commentarius* survives in the fair copy he made at Sah'â, which he completed on 11 December 1590. Monserrate concluded the book in this way:

I finished this commentary at Eynanum [Hainin] in Arabia on the feast of St Anthony of Padua in the month of June 1590. The manuscript was taken from me by the Turks at San'â, but returned again on the feast of the Eleven Thousand Virgins in the month of October the same year. I finished copying and revising the manuscript at San'â in Arabia on the feast of St Damasus in the month of December 1590.

In January he added a preface dedicating the work to Claudio Acquaviva. Later in the year he made a few additions and drew a valuable map with a table of latitudes and longitudes. *

As the time passed Paez found imprisonment harder to endure, especially when he received no letters from his friend Iturén. He had not been long enough at Goa to appreciate the length of time it took to get an answer from Spain. The letter he wrote to Iturén dated 16 February 1589 would have been sent in the flotilla leaving India for Lisbon at the beginning of 1590. If the ships had not wintered in Mozambique the letter would have reached Lisbon in June or July the same year. From Lisbon it would have been forwarded to the province of Toledo in Spain. It might, therefore, have taken nearly two years before Iturén received Paez's first letter from India, and another two before a reply reached India, let alone San'â. On 18 July 1594 Paez wrote again. The light mountain air had helped to keep him in fair health, but the hope of being ransomed that had sustained his spirits in his first year had now proved hollow. The pasha's wife, a lapsed Christian, had earlier taken pity on the priests and persuaded her husband to let them leave for Jerusalem, where he himself was going on official business. As they were on the point of setting off, an Indian had informed the pasha that if he sent them to Mocha he could exact a large sum for their redemption. At this suggestion he changed his mind. He demanded of them 20,000 ducats, put them into stricter confinement and chained them up to make sure they did not escape, giving them only black bread to eat.

The Fathers had been held captive for five years when the pasha despatched them to the slave market at Mocha on the Red Sea coast.

---

* By an unknown chance the only extant manuscript of the work is this copy made by Monserrate at San'â. Some time before 1818 it was in the library of the college of Fort William, established by Lord Wellesley at Calcutta. Later it was transferred to St Paul's Anglican cathedral, where it was discovered in 1908 on a heap of decayed books. An English translation of the original Latin was published by the Oxford University Press in 1922.

Paez rode on a camel, Monserrate, who had previously fallen from one, asked to ride an ass but was tossed off. Passing through Ta'izz, then a large walled city in the hills, they came to Mauza, at the foot of the range, and entered the southern part of the Tehama desert, which they took three days to cross before reaching Mocha.

Mocha was no place for tired and undernourished men: the heat was hellish, the drinking water infected, the air humid without a breath of breeze in the summer. At the time it was the most important port in south Yemen. From here the Fathers had once planned to sail to Massawa, for Mocha had a well-established trade with Ethiopia in gold, ivory, frankincense and mother-of-pearl, and it exported coffee to other countries as well.

When no trader in the market offered the price demanded by the pasha for the Jesuits, they were put in the galleys with three banks of oars. Their treatment was brutal and abusive. They suffered regularly from hunger and thirst; the stench and squalor of their companions on the bench bred vicious lice that kept them awake at night. Paez wrote:

> There were in the galley as many oarsmen as there were places for them to row. It was never cleaned and the dirt was unbelievable. Right through the night to dawn we were forced to remain sitting up, trying all the time to rid ourselves of the lice. As they fell on us from above we threw them into the sea; if when we were overcome by fatigue or sleep we lay down and covered our face, the lice forced us to get up and went on torturing us until morning . . . We had nothing to wear except some rags and a shirt. Our food was a handful of seeds like millet and nothing more. Now and then we were given some cloves of garlic by a Greek Christian living in Mocha. We lived like this for two and a half months exposed to the sun, water and cold.

Paez then tells how Monserrate, who fell seriously sick, was taken ashore, because the captain of the galley feared he would be held to account for his death. Brought before the Turkish Governor, the two priests were instead put to work in a quarry. With other Christian captives they were made to carry on their shoulders heavy stones to a building site; as they made their way back to the quarry they sang psalms, hymns and prayers in honour of Our Lady. 'Even the unbelievers were astonished and applauded,' wrote Paez. At night they were imprisoned again without food, their hands and feet chained and another chain round their neck attached to a stake. They kept vigil rather than slept.

This was their condition for a year until a Syrian youth, whom they had befriended before his release at San'â, was instumental in securing their ransom. He had made his way to Goa via Ormuz and informed the new Viceroy, Dom Matias d'Albuquerque, of the fate of the Fathers. Immediately the Viceroy despatched an Indian merchant to Mocha with instructions that the Jesuits were to be ransomed at any price: Philip II had previously given orders that should the whereabouts of the Fathers become known the ransom money was to come from the state treasury. Five hundred crowns were paid to the governor and a further fifty to the captain of the Turkish galley, who exacted the sum for the loss of their services.

With some regrets that such a vast sum might instead have ransomed many other captives in place of themselves, the priests sailed from Mocha and safely reached Diu, where the Guardian of the Capuchin Friary 'gave them all the entertainment that the poor Order could afford'. The Dominicans also housed them for a time, and later, when the Fathers reached Chaul, it was the turn of the Misericordia Order to give them hospitality. Finally, they reached Goa on 27 November 1596.

Three weeks later Paez wrote a short letter to the Jesuit General, Claudio Acquaviva, to whom nine years earlier he had addressed his petition to be sent on the missions. After seven years of captivity, he wrote, God had shown them great mercy rescuing them from the dark steaming benches on which they sat with heavy chains round their necks in the Turkish galley between two slaves. 'It was for the service of God that we were finally rescued,' he told Acquaviva, 'thanks to our Provincial who worked hard on our behalf.' Only on his arrival back at Goa did he learn that the General himself had also done much to get them released. Paez then asked to be allowed to set out again for Ethiopia to serve the Catholics there, 'because the only Father who now remains is so old that he can no longer read'. With this in mind he had set himself to master Arabic, which he now realized was needed to get into the country, 'because many Ethiopians who trade with the Moors speak the language and the present King also knows it'. The last paragraph in his letter concerned Monserrate: he 'was in great pain from a fall he suffered when he arrived here but now, thanks be to God, is already out of danger'.

3

Shortly after returning to Goa, Paez himself became sick and for a time hovered close to death. But after eight months he was sufficiently recovered to be sent for convalescence to the Salsette peninsula south of Goa. The Portuguese, on taking over the district in 1560, had found scores of temples dedicated mainly to Santéry, the cobra goddess. By 1580 the Jesuits had baptized here some eight thousand Indians among a population firmly attached to the Hindu religion. But in 1579 the Viceroy had proscribed all idolatrous practices in Salsette. The Hindus hoped that Philip II on succeeding to the throne of Portugal the next year would revoke the Viceroy's decree. When he did not, the five southern Salsette villages revolted and burned the Christian churches and mission stations. In July 1583 Rudolph Acquaviva, nephew of the Jesuit General, was sent to re-establish the missions, but was killed by a mob along with three other Jesuits and forty-eight native Christians.

After some months in these southern villages Paez was able to tell Iturén that the atmosphere was now greatly changed; were it not for the hostility of two highly placed persons, all the villages in his area would already be Christian. Converts were so numerous he had to build a new larger church to accommodate them. While here he showed an example of his innate tact by giving special instruction to the children of these two ill-disposed Indians, pointing out that it would benefit their careers if they could read and write Portuguese.

During his years in Salsette, Paez worked alongside Thomas Stephens, the English Jesuit who had been Superior of the mission from 1590 to 1595. With a few short interruptions Stephens remained there until his death in 1619, by which time the peninsula had become a Christian enclave among the Hindus. Like Paez, he was a missionary of exceptional talents whose fame reached England in 1599 when Hakluyt published in his *Principal Navigations* the letter he had written to his father describing the customs and languages of Portuguese India. He also compiled a Konkani grammar, the first of its kind in any Indian dialect, and wrote a epic poem, *The Christian Purâna*, which soon became an Indian classic. But Stephens was only interpreting the approach of a greater missionary than himself, Alessandro Valigano, who at this time himself influenced Paez.

Valignano had ceased to be Provincial of India in October 1587, eleven months before Paez landed at Goa from Lisbon. After a second visit to Japan he was in India again from March 1595 to April 1597 when he left for the Far East for the third time. He had organized the Japanese delegation to Rome in 1585 that had inspired young Jesuits to offer themselves for remote missions. From the beginning of his long years in authority, either as Provincial or as Visitor, in both India and Japan, he had advocated what at the time were regarded as revolutionary methods of apostolate; he had established numerous language schools and in reforming the training at the Jesuit seminary of St Paul's in Goa had insisted that the students adapt themselves to native cultures and not impose their own on others. In Japan he anticipated the formation of a native clergy and the appointment of native bishops. With his encouragement Matteo Ricci had made great progress in Peking in the face of criticism from which Valignano was always the first to defend him.

As Provincial of India from 1583 to 1587, Valigano had been responsible for the mission of Ethiopia. There would doubtless have been several meetings between him and Paez during the five months Paez was in Goa, between his return from Mocha and Valignano's departure for Japan. Possibly during these days Valignano might also have revised his earlier unfavourable opinion of Monserrate, for he had severely criticized Fr. Martins for selecting him for the Ethiopian mission: from Macao on 22 September 1589, nine months after Monserrate had left Goa with Paez, he had written in very frank terms about him to Claudio Acquaviva. Martins had presumably chosen Monserrate for the mission because of his success at the court of Akbar the Great and his experience in protocol, but Valignano had seen flaws in his character which in his view rendered him totally unsuitable for Ethiopia. 'Now it has greatly distressed me,' he had told Acquaviva, 'that the Provincial [Martins] has sent Fr. Monserrate to Ethiopia, because he possesses neither the temperament nor the character required for that mission, which in a way is

41

irrevocable, for the men sent there are unable to return to India.' Monserrate, according to Valignano's experience, was a difficult man to live with, as was well known in the community at Goa; in fact Valignano had left for Martin's information confidential notes on his character and was 'astonished that he was chosen since all this was well known': he was definitely not the person to 'bring consolation and help to the old priests in Ethiopia who had such great burdens to bear . . . . If the Lord does not impede his passage, Monserrate will cause much trouble there.' He goes on: 'When I got news of this I was unable to do anything, though I wrote to the Provincial telling him that if by any chance Monserrate had not left this year he should in no circumstances be sent.'

Since Martins would have destroyed the confidential notes left by his predecessor it is impossible to say why Monserrate was considered a difficult person to manage. Paez, during the seven years he lived with him in intimate companionship, must have learned either to suffer his failings or, as seems more likely, to have brought out in him qualities that were not evident in his own community. In his letters to his friend Iturén, Paez speaks only with affection and sympathy for his companion.

Valignano would certainly have discussed the Ethiopian mission with Paez during the months they were together in Goa. Paez's approach to Ethiopian Christianity bears all the marks of Valignano's missionary principles. As Ricci had done in China with Valignano's blessing, Paez in Ethiopia made no direct attempt to evangelize the people. Both concentrated on the court and tried to present Western Christianity in such a way that it would be acknowledged at least in certain aspects superior to the native religion.

In January 1601 Paez set out a second time for Ethiopia, leaving Bassein that month for Diu, where at the insistence of Philip III of Spain the Jesuits had established a small residence to serve as a base for the mission. The King, like his predecessor Philip II, had never abandoned hope of uniting Ethiopia to the Western Church and had ordered the Viceroy to equip six small vessels to open a passage to Massawa; in fact only two had been provided, and had set sail for Diu where Paez was awaiting their arrival. Once again plans were ruined by a storm: on the short crossing one ship was forced into Daman, a port on the Gulf of Cambay, a hundred miles north of Bombay, the other, battered and unmasted, limped into Diu.

Paez was now instructed to shift for himself. He could find no sea captain sailing to a Red Sea port who was ready to take a priest on board. In his letter from Diu he told Iturén:

> I have received letters from the Portuguese in Ethiopia in which they suggest a way in which I can enter the country. Although it is full of risks I have decided to follow it if obedience permits. They say there are no more than one thousand four hundred Catholics there and that they are so poor that most of them go about in animal skins, while the only clothing of others is a length of cotton cloth and the only covering for their head their own long hair.

Paez does not mention the route the Portuguese in Ethiopia proposed to him, but he appeared to have found another way of entering the country. He had met a merchant from the Straits of Mecca who was prepared to guide him into the interior; they would disembark secretly at night, lie up during the day and move inland under cover of darkness to escape the Turks. Then one day at Diu he made friends with some Turkish sailors and offered his services as cook in return for a passage to Massawa; but again he was disappointed.

When hope of entering Ethiopia appeared lost, Paez dreamed of searching out the Catholics of Cathay – unaware that Bento de Goes was about to leave Lahore on the same quest. He had read an ancient book, presumably the travels of Marco Polo, which gave an account of the kingdom. Here, not in Ethiopia, he believed the real Prester John of the Indies was to be found, and this seemed confirmed by merchants who had come back with stories that the ruler of the kingdom was an ecclesiastic.

This was Paez's last letter before leaving Diu. With it he sent Iturén ten rosaries made from the teeth of sea horses with the request that one should be given to his brother John.

Soon after this letter he sought out and quickly made friends with the Turkish servants of the pasha of Suakin, an island north of Massawa off the Red Sea coast, who were about to sail for home. Calling himself Abedula and dressed as an Armenian, he told them he was anxious to get back to his country but had remained in Diu for fear of falling into the hands of the Turks. Razuam Aga, the principal Turk, readily agreed to carry him safe to Suakin and from there to Cairo, where he could join a caravan to Jerusalem and then on to Armenia. Paez also asked whether on their reaching Massawa he might be allowed to go up-country in search of some goods belonging to a friend of his who had recently died. Razuam Aga assured

43

him this would be no problem and offered to pay all his expenses.

On 22 March 1603 Razuam Aga raised anchor. Paez was offered every courtesy and comfort. Just over a month later, on 26 April, he arrived safely at Massawa, the principal port of Ethiopia.

Massawa was then no more than a cluster of stone houses and a single mosque on an island in a small bay sheltered from every wind. It had been held by the Turks since its capture from Ethiopia in 1557, only a few weeks after Oviedo had landed there. Now Arab shipping, after passing through the Straits of Bab-el-Mandeb, would call there and barter their Indian artifacts for Ethiopian gold, ivory and slaves captured inland by the Muslims.

In the absence of the pasha, Paez and his friend, Razuam Aga, were lavishly entertained by a certain Mustadem, who was temporarily in command of the station and who gave Paez permission to go up-country whenever he wished in search of his friend's goods. This was a considerable concession, for the execution in 1595 of the Jesuit Francisco Abraham de Georgiis was still fresh in people's memory. *'Some gentiles,' wrote Paez to Iturén, 'were amazed at my boldness in coming this way.' Nevertheless he gathered what details he could of de Georgiis's death, learning that an Indian had disclosed the priest's identity to the Turkish captain, and that on refusing to convert to Islam he had been imprisoned. Twenty-five days later he had been taken out of the town and made to kneel while a Turk unsheathed his cutlass to cut off his head. Witnesses told Paez that at the first attempt the cutlass broke, doing the priest no harm; the second time it broke again, inflicting a slight wound; only at the third attempt did the executioner succeed. Paez was told also that they had taken the body to an island, but he was unable to discover whether it had been interred or given to the birds. For forty days, it was said, from dusk to sunrise, lights like candles had appeared in the sky above the place where the corpse had first lain. 'I wanted very much to secure the remains,' Paez wrote, 'but I could find out nothing although a diligent search had been made for them.'

On his arrival at Massawa, Paez had met a Christian from Fremona and by his means sent the Indian priest Fr. Melchior da Sylva news of his coming. For the sake of courtesy he stayed on a short time with Razuam Aga and met six other Portuguese, who unaware of his arrival had come down to the coast to enquire for letters and

* Cf. sup. 16

news from India. His leave-taking of Razuam Aga must have been difficult. The Turk, now deeply attached to him, offered to remain in Massawa until Paez had finished his business inland. The captain of the pasha's guard escorted him to the mainland along with the six Portuguese and deputed two Moorish servants to accompany them on the first stage of their journey.

Paez, clad in a Moorish burnous, was five days in the high and craggy hills before he reached Debaroa, eighteen miles south-west of Asmara. This first leg of his journey was not without incident. During a halt one night among the thorn bushes on the rough road, a sudden frightened cry woke him from his sleep. Ten or twelve paces away he saw a lion. It was driven off and the party continued on its way under a bright moon until the next day they found a safer place to sleep. Twenty-four hours later they reached a valley where they met several Portuguese herdsmen grazing their cows. They offered the travellers milk and in return were given bread, which they had not eaten for a long time. The next day, eight or ten of the herdsmen's wives came running across a mountain range; Paez wrote:

> They had first been told we were Turks, and had lain in hiding during the night, but when they learned from their husbands that one of us was a priest they came to greet us at once, asked my blessing and embraced me with many tears. The next day at evening we left these deserted regions and came to a large plain where there was a Christian village.

There they lodged for the night. Paez noted that it was the Ethiopian custom to make no charge for the first night's hospitality. The next day they reached Debaroa, a large trading centre and the key to the highland provinces of Begameder, Gojjam and Shoa, forming a large fissured plateau between six and ten thousand feet above sea level, with mountains rising as high as fifteen thousand. Debaroa was the seat of the Governor of Bahrnagash, who was temporarily absent with the Viceroy of the province. Another Jesuit, describing the same road from Massawa some years later, wrote:

> Usually all along that route there are large bands of robbers, which is what nearly all the inhabitants of the place are. Because the country is all big and high mountains and is in many parts uninhabited, and above all because it is so far from the court, they are hardly subjects of the Emperor in more than name. . . . During most of the first [four

or five] days we were climbing very high mountains among which were some cultivated fields and others of tall grass where herds of horned cattle were grazing in great numbers.

After Debaroa the road passed through the desert of Seraoe, which was infested by lions; then after ten or twelve leagues it crossed the river Mareb at a point some twelve hours' journey from Fremona, which they reached on 15 May 1603, ten days after leaving Massawa. Paez led the travellers into the church to give thanks for their safe arrival. Afterwards he took up his residence in the dwelling used by Oviedo, the round hut or *tucul* of the Ethiopian peasant, consisting only of a single room twenty palms in diameter with a roof of thatch. The captain of the Portuguese, João Gabriel, who had met Paez at Debaroa, then left for court to inform the Emperor Jakob of the Jesuit's arrival; not long afterwards Melchior da Sylva, returning from a pastoral visit to some dispersed Portuguese, departed for Goa.

The Jesuit residence at Fremona, overshadowed by high mountains, lay behind a stockade that enclosed a small school for the children of the Portuguese and the church of St George, a stone building with a simple belfry; in a side chapel the remains of the Patriarch Oviedo lay buried. While waiting for an invitation to court, Paez studied Amharic, the tongue most widely spoken in Ethiopia, and also Ge'ez, their ancient liturgical language. As in Yemen he now proved himself a keen observer of the country. Both in his letters to Iturén and later in his *History of Ethiopia* he gave exact descriptions of animals and plants centuries before any work of classification existed. He was equally precise in all he wrote about the Church, monks and the people, giving for every statement the source of his information.* In intervals of leisure he organized the translation of a brief summary of Christian doctrine, the *Cartilha*, compiled by the Jesuit Mark Georg, which was popular in Portugal, and used it for the instruction of children of mixed Portuguese and Ethiopian parentage. The news of this catechetical innovation preceded Paez to court. The Ethiopians were amazed to hear the children, who had learned the questions and answers by heart, talk of the mysteries of the Christian faith with more understanding than adults or even their own priests. Until well into the nineteenth century the only

* Cf. Appendix 2.

education open to an Ethiopian boy was some basic instruction given in church schools by priests who often were barely literate themselves.

While still at Fremona, Paez visited the monastery of Hallelujah, situated on a montain above the river Mareb, twenty miles northwest of Aksum and little more than a day's journey away. He counted six hundred cottages or hermitages still standing after the invasions but all save a few were unoccupied. The church of St Mary was in ruins; within its circuit the monks had built a much smaller church that was adequate for the reduced community.

Once twelve hundred or, as some reckoned, four thousand monks had owed allegiance to the monastery, which had ninety-one churches under its jurisdiction. Paez was told that these monks were bound only by the renunciation expressed in their vows, without any duty to enter a monastery. They could live at home or at court or in a mountain hermitage. Even within the monastery they were not hedged in by rules, but could come and go as they pleased without seeking permission of the abbot or the community. In the days of the monastery's greatness it was said that when the abbot went to court he was accompanied by a hundred and fifty monks on mules, all wearing a burnous over the monastic habit. When Paez visited it, there were only ten monks at St Mary's and a further twenty scattered abroad.

The destruction of Hallelujah was a setback for the Catholic mission, for it represented a source of monasticism common with the West. The Abbot Samuel, its founder, was in all respects comparable to the great abbots of Egypt who inspired St Benedict. An anchorite in his early days, Samuel was joined by numerous disciples for whom he wrote a rule – the first injunctions were silence and unity – that did much to promote reading, devotion and manual work in the way it was adopted in the West.

Paez observed that the churches built after the Muslim invasions were smaller and meaner than those they had replaced; they were functional buildings, mainly basilica in plan, some of them square, usually surmounted by a dome. He took measurements of the ruins of the older churches and compared his results with the descriptions given by Alvares, the chaplain to the first Portuguese embassy. Paez was later to be instrumental in restoring something of the old grandeur to Ethiopian architecture, both ecclesiastical and domestic, and it is likely that his work as an architect was the inspiration of the Portuguese palaces built at Gondar, the first capital of Ethiopia, founded shortly after his death.

The Emperor of Ethiopia had no fixed capital. As the imperial camp was the centre of administration, he and his court led a nomadic life, though he frequently retired to a summer station near Cosâ* and to a winter camp in the foothills of the mountains to the east of Gondar. When he moved from these more established bases, nothing was left behind. Normally a new site was chosen near an ample supply of firewood, and when it was exhausted another location was found. As Alvares noted, the Ethiopians were amazed to hear that in other parts of the world big cities could remain for years on the same site without any lack of firewood. 'Apart from the Emperor's camp,' he wrote, 'there is no settlement in the whole empire that deserves the name of city or even of town. They are all villages, some larger, some smaller. . . . In some provinces they are so close together that the whole countryside seems to be inhabited.' None of these places had a defensive wall or even a fence; only the villages set on ambas in areas subject to constant raids built defences, as the Jesuits did against the Turks at Fremona.

The Emperor Jakob, from whom Paez waited word to attend court, had succeeded Sarsa Dengel in 1597, the year after the death of the last Jesuit in Ethiopia. Although Sarsa Dengel in his long reign had merely tolerated the Jesuits, his successors, while warring among themselves for the crown, could almost be said to have rivalled each other in showing favour to Paez, and even in their submissiveness to Rome. Jakob, only a youth of thirteen at the time of Paez's arrival, had already been on the throne for six years. A province governor, Za Selasse, the Ras or Viceroy of Dambea and a man of pagan origins, in fact ruled the country.

When Jakob's reply reached Fremona, it was courteous. He proposed that Paez defer his visit until October when travel less tedious: in June there was risk of typhus in the highlands and malaria on the plateau, and the chill winds and damp climate lowered the traveller's resistance. Paez had no choice but to remain, for none

* Probably the modern Cerca, which on the Portuguese maps is marked to the north-west of Collela and not far from the Lake Tana. Cf. Beckingham and Huntingford, *Some Records*, 232.

could go to court unless summoned by the Emperor. However, before Paez set out, Jakob was defeated in battle and deposed by his uncle Za Dengel with the help of Za Selasse, who was quick to reassert his authority at court. The new Emperor, a large-hearted man, banished the young Jakob to the outlying province of Enarya, south of Gojjam. He might well have sentenced him to mutilation, the common penalty for pretenders to the throne, since Za Dengel had a better title to it than Jakob.*

Like many of his predecessors, Za Dengel was a man of education with a keen interest in theology. In his letter to Paez he declared that after suffering ten years of imprisonment God had made him 'the head of all things', adding in Latin that like King David he was the stone rejected by the builders that had become the cornerstone. He begged Paez to come as quickly as possible, bringing with him, if he had them, the law books of the kings of Portugal, which he was anxious to study. Presumably Paez had let it be known that he had these books in his possession. Since, in his instructions to the first Jesuits destined for the mission, St Ignatius had proposed they take with them books on civil government, Za Dengel's request can be seen as proof that Paez, either on his own initiative or at Valignano's suggestion, had made himself familiar with all the saint's directions. In fact Paez's dealings with the emperors follow exactly the lines laid down by Ignatius, which Oviedo had ignored to his cost.

Not until April 1604 did Paez leave Fremona for court. On the instructions of the Emperor, the Governor of Tigre provided a military escort to protect him from the outlaws and robbers who infested the mountain passes and lived by stealing cattle and killing travellers. It was a way of life chosen by former soldiers who preferred a free and predatory existence to the monotonous work of the fields. Feared as killers, at the same time they were admired for their bravery, fierceness and defiance of danger.

Robbers apart, the journey south had hazards enough, and was described with awe by the Jesuits who frequently made it. 'Among other mountains,' wrote one Father:

* The successor to the throne was normally nominated by the ruling Emperor from among all his male relations, whether legitimate or not. Princes not chosen by the Emperor often became leaders of revolts. Only mutilation debarred a prince from the succession.

49

travellers must cross a mountain called Lamalmon,* and before they come to the first ascent, they are at the foot of a vast high mountain called Daguça, which is as it were the foundation or pedestal of Lamalmon. It is half a day's journey to ascend this mountain, always rounding it, for it goes continually winding by very narrow paths cut along the side of the hill, with such dreadful depths and precipices looking either up or down, that if the caravan ascending happens to meet with another descending, unless they take special care where they set their feet, they are absolutely lost and tumble down those frightful depths, beating the travellers to pieces and losing the goods they carry. The commodities they generally load are India stuff and salt.'

On the summit of Daguça a large plain gave some rest to the caravans before they tackled a sharp and narrow ridge perpendicular on both sides and so deep that the bottom was not visible. This ridge led to the foot of a mountain,

almost all of it made of one entire upright rock. It was the most difficult part of all the way, and yet nature had provided a sort of steps like stairs . . . so that beasts of burden can climb and keep their feet, though they are there unloaded, for in this place there are abundance of people who live by taking the burdens off the beasts till they pass the difficulties.

This was the ascent of Lamalmon:

half a league in compass and a musket shot in diameter, formed not altogether unlike a chair without arms, for the rock on the highest part of the plain resembled the back of a chair, as perpendicular as if it had been hewn out with a chisel; and beneath it, where the rock formed a seat, was a town safe against all attacks of any enemy. From here there was a view over the whole province of Tigre with the mountains running north and north-east to form a great bow, so high that they made the mountains of Tigre look like hillocks.

From this point the route lay across the great Ethiopian plateau to the fertile and temperate regions around Lake Tana, where the Emperor was encamped.

Za Dengel had only recently returned from a campaign. He had

---

* The western extension of the Semen range, called Lamaleno on Italian maps, about twenty-five miles north-west of Buahit; at nearly 15,000 feet, the second highest mountain in Ethiopia.

routed the Galla and driven them out of a high mountain in Gojjam, where they had taken refuge with their booty – 'his men climbing or flying up the rocks cut the Galla to pieces though they made a good defence. Thus the Emperor returned to his station feared by strangers and honoured by his own people.' From the Portuguese serving with him he had learnt that Paez was well read, much travelled and able to give an account of his adventures. He was also anxious to hear two of the children that Paez had brought with him discourse on the Christian faith. He was an advocate of learning for the masses and he admired the Jesuits as educationalists.

On reaching the camp Paez found two spacious enclosures with high hedges and within them several apartments more like thatched cottages than a royal palace. The Emperor sat on a couch decorated with quilts and coverlets of brocade enclosed with silk curtains. The scene had not changed since Alvares's visit eighty years earlier. Paez was conducted to the Emperor's presence by a captain of the court. On the Emperor's right were his nobles, on his left the Superiors of certain monasteries. On approaching the Emperor, Paez raised his biretta and kissed his hand.

Za Dengel is described by Paez as a man of about twenty-six, well shaped, manly and tall. His eyes were large and beautiful, his lips thin, but his complexion somewhat tawny, a colour that Paez considered unbecoming in Europe; this apart, 'the Emperor would not have been inferior to the finest amongst us. His person was worthy of the empire he held and the majesty he represented.' Paez was commanded to sit down at the dais on which the throne stood and there conversed some time with Za Dengel, who was impressed by the Jesuit's account of his travels, with his general knowledge and with his description of Arabia. Their meeting ended when Za Dengel, already captivated by Paez's charm and humour, made a sign for him to withdraw and gave instructions for him to be generously entertained.

When the next day Paez was again summoned, the Emperor in the presence of the courtiers and monks initiated a discussion on the respective merits of Ethiopian and Roman Christianity. Then two children from Fremona were brought in and asked to recite their catechism. When the Emperor asked whether the answers the children gave were to be found in a book, he was shown the *Cartilha*. The following day Paez said Mass in a tent erected in the camp and preached in the presence of the Emperor. A day later the old

51

Empress arrived with two of her daughters and Paez was asked to preach again.

It is difficult to know the extent of Paez's mastery of Amharic at this time. He states that the more important early discussions he had with the Emperor were 'interpreted by the captain of the Portuguese', João Gabriel. But within another year he was able to read, write and speak Ge'ez and Amharic, and there is evidence that he was a fluent, simple and effective preacher. He was no proselytizer, yet as James Bruce acknowledged he was the most successful missionary ever to set foot in Ethiopia. Not only Za Dengel but persons of all ranks at court, the majority of monks only excepted, were eager to discuss with him questions of faith and Scripture. The wars against Islam and the continuing campaigns against the Galla had done much to kindle a crusading spirit in the country. Paez's presence fanned it; like Ricci in Peking, he had come to learn as well as to teach and was ready to discuss with respect the views of others.

The Portuguese who had settled in Dambea, the region on the north side of Lake Tana, now pressed Paez to visit them, for they had not seen a priest for several years. When he sought the Emperor's permission to leave court, Za Dengel objected that the swollen winter torrents made the journey difficult. Paez, however, answered that he felt obliged in conscience to meet their call. In the end he was allowed to go on condition he returned within two months; then Za Dengel, through his major-domo, offered the Jesuit some gold and grain for the journey. Paez declined the gifts but asked instead for permission to erect a church in Dambea and for sufficient land there to support the scattered and impoverished Portuguese. As long as he was receiving sustenance from the Emperor, he insisted that he needed nothing for himself. 'I did not come here,' he told the major-domo, 'to collect gold or grain, nor would I have asked for land but for the needs of the Portuguese.' Before Paez left, the major-domo was instructed to put in deposit sufficient gold for the adequate maintenance of the Portuguese.

It was not long before Za Dengel confided to him his intention of becoming a Roman Catholic. Paez was disturbed. Unsuccessfully he sought to impress on the Emperor the need for caution; he knew that when Sarsa Dengel had written to Philip II for men to cast cannons and make muskets, his enemies led by Za Selasse had spread reports that he had become a Roman Catholic and raised a rebellion. Although Paez urged Za Dengel to wait until he had received from

52

Rome answers to letters he had recently written and was about to despatch, the Emperor rejected his advice and published a proclamation ordering Sunday, not the Jewish Sabbath, to be kept as a holy day after the Roman manner. He then gave Paez for translation letters of his own composition to the Pope and the king of Portugal. In his letter to Clement VIII, dated 26 June 1604, the Emperor acknowledged the Pope's ecclesiastical supremacy and told him that he had been so impressed by Paez's learning that he had no reason to doubt his sincerity. 'We being in our empire,' he wrote, 'there came hither a Father, on whose neck is the yoke of Christ, by name Peter Pays of the House of Jesus, and brought us particular news of your Holiness, labouring to take away sin even to the effusion of your blood.' He also asked for other priests to teach the people in the way Paez had taught the children of Fremona, 'Fathers to instruct us that we may be all one heart and one body and establish the faith of Christ which was lost among the gentiles, so that peace and love may reign among us'. He did not want just any priests, but only 'virtuous and learned men who will teach us what is necessary for our souls'.

In his letter to Philip III of Spain Za Dengel asked for artisans, soldiers and again for missionaries; he was confident that with their help he could retake Massawa and evict the Turks from the coastal regions they had occupied. He desired also to drive back the Galla. In his letter to the Pope he had also asked for aid against them 'because we have in our country certain heathen enemies. If we march against these we cannot find them, for they fly, and when we return, they come in where we are not, like robbers; and therefore to destroy them we desire him [the King] to send us forces and all sorts of officers' to direct the assault on the enemy's mountain strong holds. Lastly, as a token of his earnestness, he proposed that his son should marry Philip III's daughter.

The observance of the Sabbath as the holy day of the Christian week had been an issue of great sensitivity for more than three centuries. In 1312 the Abbot Anorios of Debra Libanos, Ethiopia's most revered monastery, rising like another Nathan in the reign of Amda-Sion, had abrogated the Sabbath and excommunicated the Emperor for the first time in history for opposing his reforms. Very subtly in the name of tradition Amda-Sion had rallied the support of the opposing party, led by the monks of Debra Damo in Tigre. Anorios was condemned to flagellation and then imprisoned on the amba Guexen. But the rivalry continued and the monks of Debra

Damo used their victory to impose on the people their own doctrinal opinions and observances. Some fifty years before Za Dengel's decree his predecessor, Sarsa Dengel, had enforced silence on both parties. Now the ancient hostilities were enkindled anew. It was an issue that touched the lives of all, since on the Sabbath hunting, fishing and travelling were forbidden and no work was done in the fields. In addition there were many feastdays in honour or Our Lady, the Cross and the saints, as well as three monthly feasts in honour of St Michael, to which the restrictions applied.

Za Dengel's hasty approach to Rome had even worse consequences than Paez had feared. All that Paez could do was urge absolute secrecy, but this was violated. At court the contents of the letters were leaked. The clergy were alarmed. The climax of the discontent came when one of the Emperor's closest associates, the captain of the imperial guard, announced his intention of becoming a Roman Catholic. At this point, Ras Athanateus, the Governor of Amhara, who was later the main support of the malcontents, backed by Za Selasse, the king-maker, determined to depose the Emperor. They persuaded the monks that Za Dengel had betrayed his country, and for the second time in the Christian centuries an Abuna was prevailed upon to release the people from their allegiance.

Za Dengel now showed himself as precipitate in warfare as he had been in matters of religion. After mass desertions he was left with no more than eight hundred men. Drafted into levies, the Ethiopian soldiers had always believed they were fighting for their lord of their own free will and had the right to desert whenever they pleased. Even in battle they would shift in crowds from one side to the other when defeat seemed inevitable. Retiring now to Enarya, the Emperor was pursued by Athanateus, who in a surprise raid across the Nile seized the entire imperial wardrobe with twelve cases of gold chains and ornaments. The Emperor did not know what to do or whom to trust; he consulted Paez, who, seeing him approaching, shed tears of compassion, for he thought he looked like another David pursued by Absalom. 'See, Father,' Za Dengel said, 'how my vassals treat me. My only aim has been to strengthen religion and justice and see that the poor are not oppressed by the rich and powerful. What do you advise me to do?'

Paez urged the Emperor to retreat to some fortified position where in a short time he would be able to assemble sufficient forces to defeat not merely Athanateus but three or four rebel chiefs together. Za Dengel agreed. Then on the Emperor's insistence Paez left for Gojjam to give the sacraments to the Portuguese there who had asked for him. It was a perilous journey; apart from robbers and assassins in the hills, there was a report that the Agau, a semi-subdued people, were about to sack the place where he had his hut. However, he reached his destination safely with an escort of ten soldiers.

While Paez was visiting the Portuguese the Emperor, who had been joined by more than two thousand fresh troops, marched against the rebels. Both the commander of the Portuguese and the captain of the imperial guard believed he was strong enough to give battle in spite of his inferiority in numbers. Camping on the plain of Barcha, he attacked on the evening of 14 October 1604. Two hundred Portuguese on his right routed the enemy, but the Ethiopians on his left were slaughtered. The Emperor was unhorsed, surrounded and speared. The *coup de grâce* was given by Za Salasse himself with a javelin hurled from a distance. The body lay buried in the corner of a field until, probably at Paez's instigation, it was moved to the monastery of Dek on the island of that name in Lake Tana. Witnesses said to be beyond reproach attested that when it was exhumed it was 'as perfect and entire as when first killed, without any art used to it or embalmment. His death was universally lamented, for he was entirely beloved and the Ethiopians in their Histories call him the Chosen and Sent by God, Za Dengel.'

In Paez's absence from Fremona two more Jesuits arrived from India: Antonio Fernandes, a native of Lisbon, and Francisco Antonio de Angelis, a Neapolitan, both men of exceptional courage and ability. It had first been planned for them to accompany Paez from Diu, but it was later decided that they should remain there until they got word that the route pioneered by Paez was safe. Paez's letter announcing his safe arrival was delivered to them by the good offices of Mohammed Aga, the servant of the pasha of Massawa; he had befriended Paez on his landing and had accompanied him on the first stage of his overland journey to Fremona. At Diu, Mohammed Aga saw the two priests safely on board a ship bound for Suakin, which they reached on 24 March 1604. Here the pasha, out of friendship for Paez, welcomed them ceremoniously, giving them each a brocaded jacket, the greatest honour one Turk could do another. He then fitted out a gelva, one of the small boats used on the Red Sea, and sending his steward with them, gave him orders to see them safe to Massawa. When they were forced back by a storm, the pasha fitted out another vessel. At Massawa the commandant of the fortress provided them with a military escort until on their journey inland they met a party of Portuguese from Fremona.

The following year, early in July 1605, another two Jesuits arrived: Lorenzo Mangonio, a learned young priest, usually called Romano in Jesuit documents and in fact a Roman, and Luis de Azevedo from Chaves in Portugal, who had been Rector of the noviceship in Goa and had frequently asked to be sent to Ethiopia. Following the same route, they found on their arrival at Suakin that pasha, Paez's friend, had died and been succeeded by a 'bloody covetous villain'. The Jesuits appeased him with gifts and he agreed to conduct them to Massawa:

> Yet soon repenting he sent to stop them and seize all they had, but it pleased God his messenger came too late. The captain of the ship that brought them was not so fortunate, for the inhuman pasha laid some faked crime to his charge for which he cut off his head and seized the ship and the cargo. Not so satisfied, he privately murdered two Venetians who came in the same ship and took possession of all their effects.'

The route was now closed. Five Jesuits had suceeded in reaching Fremona between 1603 and 1605. They received no additional priests until shortly before the death of Paez in 1622.

Za Dengel was Emperor for less than a year. His defeat in 1604 was followed by a bloody civil war, during which his nephew Jakob, whom Za Dengel had deposed, briefly returned to power. In 1605 Za Selasse, with Ras Athanateus, transferred his support from Jakob to Susenyos, a nephew of Sarsa Dengel, and great-grandson of Lebna Dengel. While fighting continued, Paez did not commit himself politically. *'Judicia Dei abyssus multa'* (Many judgements of God are an abyss'), was his only comment. In the intervals of fighting he retired to Fremona to welcome the newcomers as their Superior. Then, with Fernandes and Romano, Paez returned to plead with the Emperor Jakob for the Portuguese who had suffered the loss of one hundred and fifty men in recent battles and had been deprived of their estates in Nanina in Gojjam, where Paez had visited them. This was Paez's last meeting with Jakob, who received him warmly and compensated the Portuguese with new estates at Maraba.

After two years of fighting the succession was finally decided in a day-long battle on 10 March 1607 at Dahr Zayr – probably the modern Menta Dabir – on the river Labat, ten miles north-east of the Tisisat falls. Both Jakob and the Abuna Peter were killed; Za Selasse escaped, only to be murdered a short time later by the Galla who were raiding Gojjam. His head was sent to Susenyos, who fastened it on a lance for all to see.

4

Susenyos's long reign was a period of incessant warfare. Aged thirty-two when he came to the throne, he was the son of a prince by a slave woman. This perhaps explains that, while he was deeply religious, he had no strong attachment to the Alexandrine faith; his early adherence to it was inspired more by political than by religious motives. His background was altogether unusual for a prince of royal blood. In 1573, when he was nine years old, the Galla attacked the town in Gojjam where he was being brought up, killed the adult inhabitants, including his father, and carried him off to captivity. He was rescued a year later and sent to the mother of Sarsa Dengel, who taught him Christian doctrine and gave him a sound knowledge of Scripture. When he was old enough he went back to one of his father's estates in Gojjam and there learned about warfare and hunting. On the death of Za Dengel in battle he had declared himself heir to the throne and gathered an army to assert his claim.

There is a vivid picture of Susenyos drawn by Paez, whose letters help to make him the best-known Ethiopian Emperor of the later sixteenth and early seventeenth centuries. Well shaped, with a

> long but finely proportioned visage, hazel eyes, which always had a sparkle, he smiled very amiably on all; his lips were thin, his beard black, his shoulders broad and brawny. More than average in height, he was an excellent horseman, brave, resolute, sharp-witted, well read in Ethiopian books, discreet, courteous, bountiful, martial and inured to hardships, for he was continually in arms, without one day's intermission.

A Jesuit who knew him in his later years adds details of his dress. This consisted of a 'tunic of crimson velvet down to his knee, breeches of Moorish style, a sash or girdle of many fine pieces of

58

gold, and an outer coat of damask of the same colour like a *capelhar'* – a kind of short Moorish mantle.*

Susenyos was the youngest of five sons. His eldest brother, Afa Krestos, became a monk; the second, Cela Krestos, served his brother loyally and became a fervent admirer of Paez; the remaining two, Yamana and Malka, intrigued against him and revolted, the first dying in prison, the second in battle. On and after his accession to the throne Susenyos, like his forefathers, had numerous wives and concubines, who bore him many daughters and twenty-five sons who outlived him.

When Susenyos won the throne the country was in chaos. In most provinces the governors were seeking to make themselves independent, but the new Emperor surprised them by his determination to establish his authority. Moving hastily from one province to another, he aimed to defeat rival claimants and at the same time recover territory lost to the Galla. He first attacked the Galla of Wakro, then marched against a rebel called Takluz in Tigre and cut off the nose of a monk who had assisted in stirring up the province against him. Moving into Gojjam, he slew the rebels there and defeated their allies in a three-day battle. But his domestic troubles did not end there. The body of the Emperor Jakob, slain in battle, had never been recovered. A number of young men appeared claiming to be Jakob. In one campaign against an impostor in Tigre a rumour spread that Susenyos had been killed. A grandson of the Emperor Minas then claimed the throne and was defeated by Susenyos's brother, Cela Krestos.

These campaigns lasted three years. In their annual report sent to Rome in 1609, the Jesuits refer to the seemingly endless series of revolts and conspiracies that forced the Emperor to place troops in many different parts of the country, for there was scarcely a province on whose loyalty he could depend. There was famine almost everywhere. In Tigre, which suffered as much as any province, the Ethiopians as well as the Portuguese brought their treasured belongings to the Fathers at Fremona for safe keeping. Three times the

* The only painting of Susenyos is at Akalä church in Gaynt, where he is seen praying with his son Asrate Dengel. It has not been possible to obtain a photograph of this picture, but I am nevertheless indebted to Professor Richard Pankhurst for this information. Cf. *Ethiopia Observer* (1961), IV, 381.

attempts of looters to break in were foiled. The regular stipend from the royal treasury, on which the community now depended, failed to reach them from India, but they were helped by the Emperor's brother, Cela Krestos, when his troops passed through the settlement. On one occasion the Emperor himself in the course of a campaign visited their church and was given by the Fathers a relic of the true cross, to which, as he later told them, he attributed his final victory over the insurgents.

Eventually in 1608 on 18 March, the day on which according to the Ethiopian calendar Our Lord rode into Jerusalem on the foal of an ass, Susenyos was anointed and crowned at Aksum. Here in the seventh century, when the kingdom embraced large areas of Arabia, envoys from Byzantium had reported that the sovereign surveyed his subjects from a gold-encased chariot drawn by four elephants and at court was attended by councillors carrying gilded spears. Although since then Aksum had declined in glory, the people, Semitic in origin, had proudly clung to their customs, formalized them and now re-enacted them in the rite of coronation. The ceremony gave expression to the ancient belief that the Emperor was the descendant and spiritual heir of the kings of Israel in the direct line from Menelik I, the offspring of the affair between the Queen of Sheba and King Solomon. In a dream Solomon was said to have witnessed God's favour pass from Israel to Ethiopia, a transfer confirmed by the removal of the Ark of the Covenant containing the tables of the Law from Jerusalem to Aksum, where the palace of the Queen was now a mass of rubble after the devastation of Grañ. Aksum itself had been reduced to little more than a village of some hundred houses; the only relics of its former greatness were the ruins of its old church and the numerous obelisks that surrounded it. The Jesuit Almeida, a short time later, counted twenty still standing and six or seven lying in pieces on the ground.

The Emperor's procession made its way to the new church built by Claudius with stone and mud within the shattered walls of the ancient basilica. Paez describes the occasion. Some 25,000 foot soldiers and 1,500 cavalry took part. Dressed in his crimson damask with a great chain of gold around his neck, bare-headed and seated on a richly caparisoned horse, the Emperor rode at the head of his nobles; entering the outer court, he came to the paved way before the church. Here he was stopped by the maidens of Sion, daughters of the supreme judges, who held a silken cord across his path.

Asked who he was, the Emperor replied, 'I am your king, the king of Ethiopia.'

'You shall not pass,' the maidens replied. 'You are not our king.'

Asked a second time, he said 'I am your king, the king of Israel', but again he was stopped. The third time he answered, 'I am your king, the king of Sion.'

'It is true, you are our king, the king of Sion,' came the reply. Then drawing his sword the Emperor cut the tape and at once the air resounded with acclamations of joy, volleys of small shot, the voice of trumpets, kettledrums, flutes and other instruments.

Not merely the descendant of Solomon, the Emperor was also the Elect of God, a title translated from southern Arabia and enshrined in the fourteenth-century epic *Kebra Nagast* or *The Glory of Kings*, where he is represented as a cousin of the 'King of Rome' or Byzantium. The Chronicles speak of him as a monarch of awesome power, splendid in countenance, with a God-given mission. His subjects had to prostrate themselves in his presence and keep their gaze cast down. On this day of his coronation he assumed a new name: Susenyos, as he was christened, became Seltan Sagad I. His royal insignia included a ring suspended from his right ear, a royal flag and, when on the march, a silk parasol; in procession, as on this occasion, he rode a white horse, carried a silver shield and wore a while muslin headband. He was the guardian of the peace of his people and the guarantor of civil order. No mere figurehead, he had to organize the defence of his country, lead his troops in battle and if necessary die with them. In more than theory all the land of the empire belonged to him: much of it was at his direct disposal as a reward for those who served him, whether soldiers or priests. Paez was to have dealings with him chiefly in his role as arbiter of civil and still more doctrinal disputes.

Beyond the silk tape, the new Abuna Simon, the successor of Peter who had been killed on the battlefield, awaited the Emperor's coming. In a procession of clergy and monks he conducted Susenyos into the court in front of the church where the coronation was to be enacted. Paez was not present, but he got all the details from Gabriel, the head of the Portuguese community, who witnessed the ceremony. Entering the church the Emperor heard Mass, received communion, then returned to his camp wearing his crown, which was nothing better than a 'hat with broad brims, lined with blue velvet and covered with gold and silver plates like Flower de

Luces and some false stones, for the Ethiopians, who valued gold, could not understand why genuine jewels were so highly prized in Europe'. After the ceremony the Emperor gave a number of presents prescribed by the treasury book and received in return gifts from the nobles. By ancient custom the Governor of Aksum would give the new Emperor two lions and a fillet of silk on which was written, 'The Lion of the tribe of Judah and the race of Solomon hath conquered.' This year, however, no lions were presented.

After three days festivities the Emperor moved against the rebels in Tigre. On the march he pitched his camp outside Fremona, only a few leagues from Aksum, and with a group of nobles called on the Fathers. On entering their house he removed his crown as a mark of great respect; then, as his predecessor, Za Dengel, had done, heard the children recite their catechism in the form of question and answer. He behaved, Paez told Iturén, more like a friend than an Emperor. As he left he asked whether he might attend Mass and hear a sermon in their church very early next morning. Since it was Lent, when the fast was not broken until evening, the Fathers sent after him some fish garnished in the Spanish manner and some wine made from grapes, a luxury in a country where it was commonly produced from honey. They then set to work decorating the chapel, but while awaiting the Emperor's arrival next morning a messenger came to say that urgent matters of state had detained him. Then a second messenger arrived asking the Fathers to delay Mass until midday. The meeting of the royal council continued until very late, after which the army moved on; unable to attend Mass, Susenyos sent the Fathers three hundred ducats as a token of his affection.

Three days later the Emperor sent to say where he was encamped. He proposed spending Holy Week there and begged Paez to come and preach to the court. On Palm Sunday, as Paez was about to set out, he was told that the Emperor had marched on in haste to capture some mountain passes where there had been an uprising in favour of the pseudo-Jakob. After a campaign of two months he returned at the beginning of June to his winter quarters at Cogâ, authorizing a subordinate to complete operations against the impostor, who soon afterwards was killed by his own followers and proved to be no more than a shepherd from the mountains of Bisan to the east of Asmara. On his return march Susenyos left at Fremona the Abuna Simon, recommending him to study the religion of the Jesuits and establish friendly relations with them.

In all his conversation on religious matters Paez was careful never to question the popular belief that the Church of Ethiopia owed its origin to the eunuch who in the *Acts of the Apostles* was baptized by the deacon Philip, or to destroy the legend that Queen Candace came from Aksum. The Church, in fact, had been founded in the fourth century by Frumentius, a Phoenician Christian, who had been taken captive to Aksum when the empire was at the apogee of its greatness. After serving as tutor to the Emperor's sons, Frumentius was granted leave of absence during which he was ordained bishop by St Athanasius in Alexandria. On his return to Aksum he preached the gospel with the aid of a band of missionaries on the shore of the Red Sea, in the villas of the high plateau and in all places where the Greeks had trading centres. There were Christian churches on the islands of Lake Tana by the fifth century.

Until Paez's day and after, the Church remained in a state of evangelization. It had no recognizable organization, no dioceses, no self-government; in ecclesiastical terms it was a kind of vicariate apostolic of the Church of Alexandria. On account of its non-Christian neighbours there was never a time when it was not in contact with paganism or fetishism, or free from the superimposition of Judaic customs. It took no part in the bitter battles that followed the condemnation of Nestorius at Chalcedon in 451. A decade after the Council, nine 'Roman' saints arrived in Aksum; they were not Syrians or Copts but almost certainly pre-schism Greeks sent from Byzantium. It was said that they 'rectified the faith'. Churches built in their honour in places they sanctified have preserved their cult until today; the books they brought with them were used by Paez to illustrate the authentic beliefs of the Ethiopian Church.

In contrast with other countries, Christianity in Ethiopia flourished in the sixth century; it spread to Yemen in the wake of military conquest, to southern Arabia and the further shore of the Red Sea. At this time the hospice was founded in Jerusalem for the ever-growing crowd of Ethiopian pilgrims. In thanksgiving for his victories the Emperor Kaleb donated his crown to the Holy Sepulchre. Roughly contemporaneous with this expansion was the proliferation of monasticism in Tigre with anchorites settled in the most savage solitudes. On the summit of Damo, the monastery of Debra Damo was founded by the Emperor Gabra Maskzal who, like Charlemagne, encouraged schools and revived the ancient liturgy.

The conquests of Amr ibn al As (639-44) put an end to orthodox

Christianity in Egypt. The last Catholic Patriarch, Cyprus, escaped to Constantinople. He was replaced by the Coptic Benjamin, who made a pact with Amr al As, the representative of the Calif, for the toleration of his flock. All relations with Rome and Constantinople were forbidden and the Ethiopian Church was made to accept an Egyptian Abuna nominated by the Patriarch, who moved the see of St Mark from Alexandria to Cairo. For the next three centuries Ethiopian Christians, cut off from the West, were hardly affected by the quarrels in Byzantium, which to them were no more than a distant theological tremor.

Although now officially tied to the schismatic see of Cairo and enfeoffed in the Coptic Church, Ethiopia preserved an independent and entrenched doctrinal independence. In the monasteries and in the cultivated court circles no doctrinal jurisdiction was given to the Abuna, whose ignorance of the language and customs of the country made him despicable in their eyes; they had their own doctors and saints, to whom Paez was to appeal. For a long time the country remained doctrinally more akin to Byzantium than to Cairo, although the Coptic Abuna, as Paez was to discover, had always around him sycophantic followers. A crisis occurred in 820 when an Abuna sent by Cairo was turned out of Aksum because of his dissolute life. For more than a hundred years, during the reign of five Patriarchs in Cairo, there was no bishop in Ethiopia.

In the early eleventh century Ethiopia became the asylum of Coptic Christians persecuted in Egypt by the Calif Hakim. For another long period the country was without a bishop until in 1093 Cairo appointed the Abuna Georgiis, who caused indignation by amassing riches and pressuring parishes for money. Eventually he also was expelled by the Emperor, who in 1331 tried to gain independence of Cairo and establish a hierarchical constitution for the Church. The attempt, inspired by a monk of Jerusalem in contact with the Crusaders, came to nothing. The Coptic Patriarch, anxious to curry favour with the Calif, persuaded him that the plan was against his interests, for it would ally Ethiopian Christians with those of the West. During the fourteenth century, four or five hundred descendants of the Egyptian *emigrés* built the rock churches of Lalibela.

A hundred years later there was a fresh movement towards union with the Church of Palestine, but again nothing came of it. The same period saw a revival of the Church, associated with the monk Takla Haymanot, who converted to Christianity the pagans in Damot and

Shoa and in the region of the Nile. The grant of one third of the territory of the empire to the Church led to exorbitant greed among the clergy. Debra Libanos, where Takla Haymanot died, became an ant-hill of monks counted by the thousand; they swarmed out seeking solitude in the remote parts of the country. Among Takla's imitators was Eustathius of the monastery of Hallelujah in Tigre, which Paez visited in his first months at Fremona.

A last attempt to break with Cairo was then made. At the request of the Emperor Amlâk, a Syrian Bishop was sent from the Patriarch of Jerusalem and came accompanied by a party of Dominican Friars. Their arrival coincided with the presence of St Louis, King of France, in Egypt, but this approach was formally rescinded by Amlâk's successor; he expelled the Dominicans, whose memory was still fresh among the people in the sixteenth century. Then the Patriarch of Cairo made an effort to revive the Coptic faith in Ethiopia. This led to a period of stiff formalism that lasted until the coming of the Jesuits and did much to impede their success. It was most apparent in the rigorous enforcement of the days of fasting, which were more severe and more numerous than in any other Christian Church. The ordinary Amhara, or Ethiopian of the central provinces, was supposed to fast a total of one hundred and sixty-five days in the year, and the devout man some two hundred and fifty. It was the foremost obligation undertaken by a Christian, and began for children at the age of seven. After it came the observance of the Sabbath and the duty to contribute to the support of the local church. With the formalism went a looseness of morals. At court licentiousness was accepted as the right of kings, polygamy and divorce as necessary to meet the weakness of human nature. None of the learned men or monks surrounding the Emperors condemned them in the name of Christian morality. Fornication and adultery, though forbidden, were generally excused or accommodated. Only incest was vehemently reproved, and there was rigid enforcement of the ban on marriage up to the seventh degree of kinship.

This was the time that Anorios, the Abbot of Debra Libanos, excommunicated the Emperor and started the bitter controversy on the observance of the Sabbath which split the Church. However, the tenuous links with Jerusalem were maintained throughout the fourteenth century and led to the Ethiopian presence at the Council of Florence.

In the area of Fremona, even before the Emperor's visit, the

Fathers were established in the confidence of the people. They were respected for their truthfulness and their fidelity to their promises, which they did not have to re-enforce with oaths. They were admired also for their total lack of vindictiveness in a society influenced by Jewish customs. Their patently good lives impressed their neighbours, who would ask naïvely what methods and medicines they used to preserve their chastity. As one monk admitted to them, their own priests resembled more the Pharisees, leading dissolute lives and at the same time wanting to be thought good men.

Before his coronation the Emperor had given the Jesuits a fine property for a church and settlement at Gorgora. This area of low-lying land that borders on Lake Tana rises into a rocky promontory and forms a peninsula running out into the lake.* Paez settled Fernandes and Romano there, leaving for the present the other two Jesuits at Fremona. Monks came frequently from their houses on Lake Tana, the most flourishing centre of Ethiopian monasticism, on visits to the Fathers in their new residence. The main theme of their talks was the precise nature of Christ.

It was the monophysite doctrine of one nature of Christ, derived from Alexandria, that for centuries had separated the Ethiopian Church not only from Rome but from all other patriarchates that had accepted the creed of Chalcedon in the year 451. In the period preceding these discussions, the doctrine had been differently interpreted, elaborated and refined by divergent schools of monks. As a starting point for their talks Paez translated the chapter of Cardinal Bellarmine's famous book of *Controversies* on the dual character of Christ as God and man, and copied out alongside it passages in a similar sense from the Ethiopian codices. He did the same on the question of the creation of souls, which had a direct bearing on the subject. Paez had discovered that most Ethiopians were generally taught to believe that the soul was not created by God but had its origin, like the body, in human generation.

Since Paez was often engaged at court, the role of the theologian

---

* Bruce wrote of Gorgora that 'nothing can be more beautiful than this small territory, elevated but not to an inconvenient height above the water which surrounds it on all sides except the south. The climate is delightful and no fevers or other diseases rage here. The prospect of the lake and the distant mountains is magnificent beyond European conception, and nature seems to have pointed out this place for pleasure, health and retirement.'

fell largely on Fernandes, who already at Goa had studied the Ethiopian faith. In a letter of 3 June 1610 to the Jesuit Superior there he regretted that no commentary on the errors of the Ethiopian Church had yet been published. There had been one in preparation before his departure, and at that time it had required no more than six months' work by a Jesuit not heavily engaged before it could be made ready for the press. Fernandes was unwilling to believe that the expense of production was the cause of its delay. Now he listed what he himself considered the main points of difference between the Ethiopian Church and Rome, which he had learned in his conversations with monks and clergy and from his reading of their books. In his view they wrongly believed St Leo had taught that Nestorius maintained there were two Christs, though not two Persons, a theological nicety that scarcely concerned the faithful. What touched them most sensitively were the peripheral practices that had been rigorously adhered to since the Alexandrine Christians had been isolated from the West; others were associated with the ceremonies of the old Judaic law, such as abstinence from pork, hare and non-scaly fish, the uncleanliness of women after menstruation and on giving birth, circumcision of both sexes and the holiness of the Sabbath. The sacrament of baptism, which was given once in the rest of the Christian Church, was renewed with them whenever a son had sexual intercourse with his mother or a youth entered a monastery, and whenever a Christian who had gone over to Islam returned to his former faith. In the days of Grañ many had become Muslims to save their lives. (The descendants of some of them form today the small Amhara Muslim population of the highlands, who know little or nothing of the teaching of the Prophet, and never journey to Mecca or observe Ramadan.)

These were the common errors. In addition, owing to the freedom allowed believers, there were others not others universally held, mainly concerned with the nature of the soul. Fernandes had met individuals who held that the soul was part of the Holy Spirit or of Adam's own soul, or composed of the four elements. Others believed that in heaven God, although a Spirit, could be seen with the bodily eyes.

As Paez soon found out, it was not this or that particular belief that formed the obstacle to reunion with Rome. It was rather the pride of the people in their old religion, which they had preserved without change for eleven hundred years. He knew that little was to be gained by a direct confrontation with their old usages. His approach was different from that of Oviedo before him and of Alfonso Mendes who followed him, yet in all points he observed the guidelines laid down by St Ignatius for the first band of Jesuits assigned to Ethiopia. His plan was slowly to bring the Emperor and persons of influence to recognize the superiority of Western Christianity in the hope that customs not consonant with it would in time be abandoned for more orthodox practices.

Paez understood that Ethiopia, so close to Arabia and assaulted in the north by fanatical Muslims, was rightly proud of its adherence to Christianity – curious though it was in form, corrupt in some points of doctrine and extravagant even in much that it maintained of orthodox usage. From his experience in Yemen, Paez realized that changes in matters of religion occur only slowly in Oriental nations that have been cut off from communication with the West. He understood also that the Ethiopians were wedded to their ancient practices which for more than eleven centuries had been the props of Christianity among the people. He looked for what he could commend. Most of all he appreciated that the Amharic conception of God lacked complexity, since the clergy had avoided anything comparable to the systematic theology that had developed in the West, convinced that too deep an enquiry into God's nature was not far removed from blasphemy. Their God was the God of the psalms, the all-knowing, almighty and all-merciful Lord of heaven, earth and angels, and the King of Kings. Paez saw this in the constant awareness among the people of the presence of the divinity, whose name was invoked many times a day in social intercourse. In their extravagant devotion to Our Lady they needed convincing that Rome also honoured the Virgin. But at the centre of all external worship, their belief in the Eucharist, though not free from much unsound theology and superstitious accretions, remained the distinctive feature and in its way even recaptured something of the atmosphere of the third- and fourth-century Church. Here he found much to admire. Their belief in the Real Presence was at one with that of Rome, and Paez found more compelling proof of this in the hagiographical literature of Ethiopia – which gave an insight into the mind of the most venerated ascetics – than in any liturgical formula. He understood how the Portuguese priests at first caused scandal by using thin white wafers at Mass, which the people believed were made from the brains of the hare or camel, animals that they held in abhorrence.

Paez's sympathetic approach is well illustrated by a passage in his *History* concerning Ethiopian practice. He writes:

They use fermented bread for the consecration, and for the making of this they have a little chamber outside the church. Here nothing is kept but what is necessary for making the bread and wine which they use, but this is where one of the Brothers [Paez seems to be speaking of a monastic church] grinds the flour, not without much labour when a good deal of bread is required, for they never employ a horse-mill. Sometimes, however, they entrust the grinding to some widow or respectable married woman who lives near the church. When the hour comes for making the bread – this is always shortly before Mass, and they are greatly astonished that we do not make our hosts every day – a priest comes along and kneads the dough with leaven. If there are only a small number of communicants, he makes a cake [*fas bum pão*] about the size of the paten and a little more than a finger-breadth thick and as broad as may be necessary, since they never use more than one loaf to consecrate with, except on certain great feasts when they make three. This loaf or cake is marked with five little crosses by means of a stamp in that form, and immediately afterwards he makes a number of other small cakes which are [later on] distributed to everybody as blessed bread [*como pão bento*]. Then he bakes the whole batch in a great clay bowl, and when they are baked, he puts the loaf to be consecrated in a little copper basin, while the others are kept in a basket which is set apart for the purpose.

At the same time Paez had his doubts about the validity of the Ethiopian Eucharist because of the way they produced what passed for wine. 'In the same chamber,' he continues,

a little before Mass the wine is made from raisins in the following way. They take the dry raisins which are kept there all year round and after washing them they put as many as seem sufficient into a basin, squeezing them into pulp with the hand in a fresh supply of water. This is strained through a clean cloth, and in some churches where the store of raisins is apt to run short they pour in so much water – so at least I was told by the Brothers – that it is hardly more than just reddened, though the raisins are always black. What is more, the same Brothers assured me that frequently, using only four or five raisins, they poured in so much water that it served not only to say Mass with, but to communicate a number of people, for communion

69

is given in both kinds. From this it is clear that they do not validly consecrate, since there is no wine there, but only water. But for all that they say the words of consecration and bow down to adore.

Nevertheless he was full of admiration for the decorous behaviour of the people during the celebration of the Eucharist. They neither talked nor laughed nor spat. Dogs were rigorously excluded from their churches and, like the Mohammedans in their mosques, every worshipper – including the Emperor – took off his shoes on entering the building. Paez noted also the way travellers riding past a church dismounted and led their horses past the building by the bridle. Many other passages in the *History* further illustrate his lack of prejudice in his approach to the Ethiopian Church.

It was, then, with a mind both open and prepared to compromise that Paez in 1610 answered the Emperor's summons from Gorgora to his court at Cogâ, close to where the Blue Nile leaves Lake Tana. Since the rains had been heavy the Emperor instructed him not to attempt to cross the lake but to work his way in a *tankua* round the shore keeping close into the bank. These *tankua* or reed rafts, the traditional form of transport on Tana, were bound together by strips of bark from the fig tree and propelled by two poles of shambuko, a type of bamboo that grew on the shore. In deeper water rowing was done with a shorter pole grasped in the centre, for the Waitos, the tribesman living by the lake and the only people able to navigate the craft, did not know the use of a bladed oar. These people had settled here earlier than the Amhara and, though regarded as inferior by them, had never been driven out, for they alone could manage the water traffic and transport. Paez was amazed that the Amhara were content with a vessel of this kind, which was 'as thick as a man's arm and a fathom in length', and was alarmed lest the motion of the water or, worse, a hippopotamus should overturn it. In the account of his journey Paez assures future travellers on Tana that 'certainly there are no tritons or sirens in the lake', although when striking across a small creek, a hippopotamus did make for his *tankua*. Fortunately when they reached the further bank the hippopotamus left them for lack of water.

The bulk and behaviour of the hippo intrigued both Paez and other Jesuits who encountered it. It was then unfamiliar in Europe, although as early as 58 B.C. Aemilius Scarus, then serving as aedile or officer of public buildings in Egypt, had brought the first hippopotamus to Rome, where a canal was constructed to receive it. The creatures became a common sight there in the next two centuries, when they were captured for combat in the arena. Although there is an obscure reference to the dissection of one by Fabio Colonna in Italy in 1616, the Jesuits took delight in describing the hippopotamus to their brethren in Spain, for they could be certain that they had never seen one in captivity at home.* Paez, however, does not seem to have sampled its flesh as did another Jesuit, Jeronimo Lobo, whose observation of its conduct is more detailed than Paez's. Writing ten or more years later, Lobo explains:

[The] hippopotamus or river horse grazes upon the land . . . yet is no less dangerous than the crocodile. He is the size of an ox, of a brown colour without any hair, his tail is short, his neck long, and his head of enormous bigness: his eyes are small, his mouth wide, with teeth half a foot long, he hath two tusks like a wild boar, but larger, his legs are short and his feet part into four toes. It is easy to observe from this description that he hath no resemblance to a horse, and indeed nothing could give occasion to the name but some likeness in the ears, and his neighing and snoring like a horse when he is provoked. His hide is so hard that a musket fired close to him can make only a slight impression, and the best tempered lances pushed forcibly against him are either blunted or shivered unless the assailant has the skill to make the thrust at certain parts which are more tender. There is danger in meeting him, and the best way is, upon such an accident, to step aside and let him pass by. The flesh of this animal doth not differ from that of a cow, except that it is blacker and harder to digest.†

On reaching Cogâ, Paez was greeted by the Emperor, who invited him to dine next day. He describes how two tables were

---

* The part of the building in the London Zoo occupied by the hippopotamus was built in 1850 to accommodate a young animal captured in the White Nile, near Ubayd. It is believed to have been the first hippopotamus imported alive into Europe since the exhibitions in the arenas of ancient Rome.

† This and other extracts from Lobo's *Itinerario* are taken from Dr Samuel Johnson's *Voyage to Abyssinia*, a translation from the French, which itself was made from a Portuguese text that has been lost. Johnson would appear to have shortened Lobo's narrative, which can be read in full in the text established by M. G. Da Costa and translated by Donald M. Lockhart (Hakluyt Society, 1984).

placed in an anteroom, a small one for the Emperor and a larger one for his guests, neither covered with damask cloth nor laid out with plate. Between the two tables hung a curtain, for protocol would not allow the Emperor to be seen eating except by two or three attendants. First, ten women entered; they were dressed like the servants of great ladies in long and wide gowns of coarse cotton tied with a sash and falling in large folds to the ankle. They brought in *macobos* of multi-coloured straw containing twenty or thirty *apas* at least half a yard in diameter and made of a mixture of wheat, peas and teff. Other women followed with several kinds of pottage in black earthenware porringers. The tables were then covered with *apas* which served as napkins, dishes and food. After this came the raw beef, which was laid on the *apas* and cut either by the Emperor himself or by one of his attendants, who put large portions into his mouth. This custom was observed well into the twentieth century by the Empress of Ethiopia, who was still fed behind silk curtains by her slaves.

On this occasion the Emperor confirmed a grant of land to the Jesuits at Gorgora in the traditional manner, so that they could enjoy its immunities in perpetuity. This was done through an *azage* or judge, who went around the boundaries with minstrels calling the people to witness to the landmarks as they were set in place. Goats were then killed and their heads buried as further markers.

From the court Paez wrote to the Emperor's brother, Cela Krestos, then Viceroy of Tigre, to seek his intervention on behalf of the Jesuits at Fremona, whose alms from India had been confiscated by the Turks at Massawa. The Viceroy threatened penalties, got back the alms and, with the intention of making the Jesuits and their school independent of revenues from abroad, donated land that included five villages whose inhabitants had left owing to the ravages of war. It was hoped that they would now return and that the Jesuits as their overlords would derive a steady income from the feudal dues. Then Cela Krestos persuaded the Emperor to ratify the gift in perpetuity, as had been done at Gorgora.

The Christians of the Cogâ region had defaulted in their payment of tribute on the ground that they had suffered devastation from the Galla. In an attack on them about this time, the Emperor slew three hundred and took another twelve hundred captive. Paez, who was still at court, pleaded with Susenyos to show clemency to the rebels, both individuals and groups. Distressed at the sight of so many fine looking boys and girls taken into captivity, he argued that unless they were released their country would even be more exposed to the Galla and ultimately denuded of its population. Against the majority of his councillors the Emperor released the captives and astonished the court. *Hic est verus et genuinus apostolus*, it was said of Paez. The Emperor was reported to have remarked, 'Whatever I set eyes on him, I look upon an angel.' Moreover Paez, in Susenyos's estimation, fulfilled the Amharic ideal of the good man: he practised good works and observed the ritual fasts and feasts, but most important of all, he did not interfere in the lives of others. The Emperor and courtiers carried on as they had always done. All agreed that he was incapable of causing offence, and a number of governors, taking their lead from the Emperor, released the prisoners they held in their own provinces. On this visit also Paez strengthened an already firm friendship with the Emperor's half-brother, Bella Krestos, a keen and well-read theologian.

On his side Paez found it easy to give his affection to the Amhara: there was much in their character that appealed to him. He found the 'learned men' at court intelligent, mentally alert and eager to listen. Called *dabtara*, these courtiers were neither clergy nor monks but students who had followed a course of studies well beyond the requirements for priests. Their curriculum included religious dances, the study of Ge'ez, a vast corpus of ecclesiastical chants and some twenty or more religious books. Their course of reading was seldom completed, but they might at the same time study herbal medicine or writing. Mainly they were to be found at court where they were chroniclers, poets, scribes or choristers; and when such positions were unavailable they might earn their living by cultivating the land or practising medicine. Neither ordained nor distinguished by dress, they were respected for their education and also frequently feared for the magical powers that the peasants attributed to them. A group of these men formed part of the permanent entourage of Cela Krestos, who placed them at the service of the Jesuits in their work of translation. They would appear to have been more open-minded than the monks but unlike them exercised no political influence. At court also were the supreme ecclesiastical office holders: they included the guardian of the canonical hours (the chief churchman at court), the Emperor's chaplain, the head of the *dabtara* and 'the chief of the learned men'. Together the four served as supreme judges at court. Paez found these persons quick to

73

absorb the new learning he purveyed, though perhaps not as deeply as they themselves believed. A born diplomat, selected for the mission even before his ordination to the priesthood, he appreciated their innate courtesy and charm. He understood their bow and knew that the kiss given to strangers like himself was not an act of obsequiousness but a gesture of courtesy. Always he offered them the same hospitality that he received from them.

On this visit to the Emperor, Paez was struck down with fever. In his distress the Emperor sent daily messengers to enquire after his condition. There were a few Portuguese at court, probably in the capacity of military advisers. Tactfully, when Paez recovered after ten days, he started regular *colloquia* with them on religion. Soon a number of nobles joined them, moving their tents closer to his. In this way a series of religious conferences was initiated that became a feature of life at the imperial court. When the Emperor moved on, Paez sought leave to return to Gorgora, but Susenyos insisted that he remain with him. Often Paez was summoned for discussions with the Emperor; often also, when he had his own business to transact, concerning either Fremona, Gorgora or the Portuguese, he sought an audience of the Emperor and was made to take a seat beside him.

Although there were still stirrings of rebellion in the remoter provinces, the principal military effort was now directed against the Galla. Year after year Susenyos sought to protect the highlands of Ethiopia against their incursions. The Chronicles record his campaigns. On his accession the Galla were already encroaching onto the plateau, where they abandoned their nomadic life and became cultivators of the soil. Between 1606 and 1617 they made intermittent raids into Gojjam and Begameder but for the most part were held back or worsted in battle. When in the nineteenth century renewed contact was made by Europeans with Ethiopia, the Galla were found to be settled in vast areas of the country, and were finally subdued and integrated only by Menelik II in the 1890s.*

Distinguished from the Ethiopians by their darker skin, the Galla did not have the Negro's thick lips or flat nose. At this time all were

* There is a short earlier account of the Galla written in 1593 by an Ethiopian called Bahrey, probably a monk, which is valuable but less detailed than Almeida's. A translation of Bahrey's work is printed in Budge's *History of Ethiopia*, vol. 2, 603-17.

heathen or 'rather neither Christian nor Moors. They worshipped no idols and took no account of God.' Generally their physique was good and they were courageous in battle. When in 1611 the Emperor's camp was threatened, Paez was sent for protection with a military escort to the amba Guexen on the borders of Shoa. By no means the most impregnable of scores of such precipitous mountain fortresses, it was here that, until the accession of Claudius, the Emperor's sons and their descendants were confined for life to prevent them from asserting a claim to the throne while he was campaigning on distant frontiers. Almost round in shape, it rose steeply on all sides from the low-lying meadows. On the grassy summit was an abundant supply of food and clear water. Its two churches, recently sacked by Grañ, were served by monks, beneficed clergy and choristers. For twelve days, until the danger was over, the monks and the entire population of the amba showed Paez every kindness.

On his return to camp, Paez accompanied the Emperor and his brother Cela Krestos in the field, holding theological discussions with them in their tents during halts on the march or in the intervals of fighting. Wherever he went that year the Emperor seized for his army all the booty he could get, for famine raged in most provinces: 'old people, and nobles among them, were like walking skeletons'. Prayers were ordered throughout the kingdom. In addition to famine there were floods, thunderbolts and acute frosts that destroyed the germinating seed. 'All were scared,' writes the Jesuit chronicler, 'by the noise of raging gales; trees were uprooted and people saw rocks flying through the air and giving out sparks of fire as they collided.' In his first campaign the Emperor won a victory in the open plain and captured the Galla's herds of cattle, after which the enemy split up into small groups and fought from caves in the rocks. Before the engagements the Ethiopians were amazed to see the Portuguese fighting with Susenyos go to confession to Pedro Paez.

These Portuguese formed only a very small handful of Susenyos's strength. When he had mustered all his forces he could put some thirty or forty thousand men into the field, all but four or five thousand of them infantry. Apart from fifteen hundred jennets, the rest of the horses were jades and nags. Only seven or eight hundred horsemen wore coats of mail and helmets; their principal arms in battle were *zargunchos*, half-length lances with thin shafts, and their protection consisted of round shields, nearly a yard in diameter and made of buffalo hide. Chieftains alone carried swords, which they seldom used except on ceremonial occasions; the rest wielded clubs called *bolotâs* and short daggers for fighting at close quarters. As a Jesuit wrote, 'They have more than one thousand five hundred muskets but not more than four or five hundred musketeers are found on expeditions, and most of them have so little skill that they cannot fire more than once in any action.'

Generally speaking they were good troops, inured to hardship in all seasons. However, the forces drawn from the Christian highlands suffered from their strict adherence to the rigorous laws of fasting, which impaired their stamina in the prolonged Ethiopian Lent, the height of the campaigning season, when they could neither eat nor drink until midday even though they had been at work or on the march since dawn. Both the Muslims and the Galla regularly attacked at that time or on Wednesdays or Fridays when the same rules applied. All the same, as Almeida wrote, 'in war they grow old, for the life of all who are not farmers is war'. Their pay was a grant of land which they enjoyed as long as they were in service.

In spite of their strength in numbers, the Ethiopians had a great fear of the Galla and fought well against them only when they were inspired by the Emperor's example. Unlike their enemy they were left to themselves to learn the arts of war and to provide their own equipment. In battle their only tactic was to overwhelm or envelop the enemy by superior numbers. Primarily peasants, they were man for man no match for the fiercer and more professional Galla who, as Paez explained, had to prove their prowess by smearing their bodies with the blood of an enemy (this was thought to make them invisible by night) or by cutting off his foreskin. When they marched it was always at night, yet they were able to cover twice the distance that the Ethiopians did in a day. In this way they could surprise their enemy in a sudden raid. With them came their women-folk whose task it was to fortify the encampment, raise ramparts, dig trenches and load the oxen. Like the Ethiopians their fighting troops used both the javelin and club, but fought naked down to the belly. Paez held that they had the morals of savages, but unlike Fernandes he believed that they worshipped one God whom they called Oacha.

During the 1611 invasion the Galla reached Tigre. Some five thousand of them splitting into small contingents spread across the province. The Jesuit house at Fremona became a refuge for the neighbouring people who had not already gone into hiding among the rocks. No longer the collection of mud huts on a hill above the confluence of two streams, which gave the district the name of Maegoga or Roaring Waters, the settlement had been moved by Paez to a crest to the west of the same hill, where it was less exposed to roving bands of robbers. There a house of stone and mud had been built with a strong enclosure in the style of a fort. On its completion some years after these raids, the compound contained seven or eight bastions with high curtain walls and two courtyards, one of which adjoined the house, the second the church. Another curtain wall protected it from musket shot from another crest of the same hill, although owing to the incompetence of the Ethiopians with firearms little was feared from this quarter. Manned by twenty or thirty Portuguese armed with muskets and a small cannon, the place was considered impregnable. The town, scattered all over the hill, was, like the residence, unique for it contained many houses of stone, which could easily be dug in slabs from the mountainside with nothing more than a light lever.

For eight days the invaders sat threateningly outside Fremona; others attacked Aksum where, as Grañ had done before them, they stabled their horses in the church. A well-known monk who was taken with four young aspirants had his ears, nose and private parts cut off while the four young monks with him were strangled.

Paez had no option but to join the Emperor in the field. Always remarkably cheerful, he was, as Bruce wrote, in great request among the young men of Ethiopia who spent much of their time in high-spirited conversation in the camp. His command of the language must have been near-perfect for the Amhara savoured the smart repartee and the double-edged remark more than the incongruous situation. Good tales and extempore songs were the staple entertainment of the troops on the march. When the Emperor moved, the entire court, clergy included, went with him. There was as little pacifism in Ethiopian Christianity as there had been in Europe when Urban II proclaimed the First Crusade at Clermont in 1085. Though forbidden to shed blood, priests gladly supported warfare that was mainly directed against Muslims, pagans and Judaic people, or against rebellious chieftains whose sins merited divine chastisement. They carried the ark or altar with them to the battlefield and when the fight was joined sustained the spirit of the army with their prayers – all this was to serve their Emperor, who as the 'Lion of Judah' was their divinely appointed warlord.

Usually the army and its entourage contained more women than men, including the Queen, noble ladies and wives of the chief captains, with their households and families; every soldier had with him one wife or more, who took care of the commissariat, for in Ethiopia, as Almeida explains, 'there is no biscuit or other food that keeps for many days, and so they have to make their *apas* every day, and for this they must grind meal which is entirely women's work'. It was the same with the honey wine, which the women made and carried. There were also merchants in the train selling cloth and other goods, 'so that when ten thousand soldiers march, the number in the encampment is usually over thirty thousand, and when the Emperor marches with this entire force, the whole multitude is over a hundred or a hundred and twenty thousand'.

The camp resembled a forest of tents. In the centre were the five tents of the Emperor, which formed the precincts of his court. Then, beyond an open space, the tents of the Queen, the commanders and churchmen: an impressive sight at night when all the camp fires were lit. This was the capital of Ethiopia where Paez also pitched his tent and held theological discussions. When camp was broken it was as if the empire was on the move. While passing through friendly territory there was no order of march except for the vanguard commanded by the marshal, who selected the ground for the next camp and then planted his standard where the Emperor was to pitch his tents. In front of the Emperor himself went trumpets and kettledrums. Always riding a she-mule, he mounted and dismounted in his tent. On his way he wore a crown and used a silk umbrella, but Susenyos did away with the cloaking curtains used by former emperors, in the belief that his visible presence inspired his troops against the Galla. 'When the enemy is near at hand,' Almeida wrote, 'the army proceeds in more order and closer formation, with close squadrons.' The wings then extended and the Emperor took up his position in the centre.

After the first series of campaigns against the Galla, Susenyos moved his camp from Cogâ, leaving nothing behind to mark the place. After a brief stay at Dehana, on the south of the river Takaze, he moved to Dancaz, where he established what was to become a fairly permanent court. It was a fine position and about half a day's journey from the Jesuits at Gorgora. Almeida gives a detailed description of the site, a platform of land, as he calls it, a little over a league long and a little less wide at the summit of a long steep ascent. Mountains cut away almost perpendicularly ringed it round, so that it formed a natural position 'for a fine city to be built there if it had been in Europe: it contained many springs and streams . . . and meadows where much grass grows on which all kinds of cattle graze'. Wheat and barley were sown and reaped everywhere. When Almeida visited it some ten years after it had been established most of the trees had been cut down for firewood or building and never replaced, so that it was only a matter of time before it had to be abandoned. In Paez's days it had as many as eight or nine thousand thatched dwellings. It was here that he lived for the greater part of his years in Ethiopia.

5

Paez and his fellow Jesuits never doubted the Emperor's sincere affection for them. 'His devotion to us,' wrote the compiler of the annual report for 1611, 'grows daily, and he particularly admires the way we observe the regulations of our Church.' It was clear to them that Susenyos was drawn to Rome not only by his admiration for Paez but also by the hope of military assistance against the Galla. At the same time, however, the Emperor had reason to fear for his throne if he were to avow openly his allegiance to the Pope. While he sought tactfully to steer a middle course, avoiding a confrontation with the established Church, he found it increasingly difficult to show impartiality to the Jesuits, whom he applauded instinctively whenever they got the better of their opponents in the religious discussions at court.

In 1611 a letter from Philip III, dated 15 March 1609, reached Dancaz. In it the King expressed his wish to cultivate the Emperor's friendship, suggested that he should write frequently and asked him to continue his protection of the missionaries and the Portuguese community. Later the same year or perhaps in the first month of 1612 Susenyos received a letter from Pope Paul V, to whom he had written in October 1609 shortly after his accession. Although this letter appears to have been lost, there is a reference to it in the Jesuit report on Ethiopia for the year 1609. The Emperor had asked for thousand Portuguese troops, but as no answer was received he had written again on 6 June 1610. When he was handed the Pope's reply he read the letter carefully, burst into tears and kissed the parchment. The elegant characters fascinated him and also the papal seal depicting St Peter gathering in a netful of fish. The Pope praised the Emperor for his zeal for the Christian cause and gave him some hope of military aid. 'As you asked us to do,' he wrote, 'we have commended the present needs of your kingdom to our very dear son in Christ, Philip the Catholic and mightly King of the Spains, who, we trust . . . will give you effective help; and we have commanded our Apostolic Nuncio, who is with His Catholic Majesty, to solicit diligently what you ask.'

These letters and the interest Cela Krestos and his half-brother Emana Krestos, were taking in Western Christianity made Susenyos anxious to forge closer ties with Rome. With his approval Fernandes had visited Gojjam to spend some weeks in theological discussions with Cela Krestos, who had been transferred there from Tigre. Fernandes wrote on 12 March 1611:

> I reached Gojjam on the tenth day after leaving the royal encampment. All the time I was with Cela Krestos he showed me great kindness: he enquired into many points of our belief and practice and asked several learned men to join our talks. He admitted that according to both the gospels and their own books our doctrine of the two natures of Christ was correct. Since he wanted further clarification on this, he interrupted the business of state and took me into a more private room of his palace, where we resumed our talks the entire day long, continuously, over several days. We dealt with almost every question raised by theologians.

In the same year the Emperor marched against the Galla in Gojjam. The campaign was important, for the province's contribution of gold to the imperial treasury was second only to that of Enarya, and it provided also, as part of its revenue, some three thousand horses which Susenyos needed for his army. Already the north-west of the province was occupied by the Agau, who were only nominally the Emperor's subjects, and it was now vital that the rest of Gojjam should be saved from the Galla. Its inhabitants were poor soldiers, and it was probably for this reason that Susenyos had transferred Cela Krestos there from Tigre.

During the campaign there was an occasion when the Emperor was alone with Cela Krestos and Pedro Paez. Their talk turned to the Roman faith. Paez agreed that the time had not yet come for the Emperor to declare himself a Catholic: both had witnessed the revolt that had followed Za Dengels's precipitate conversion to Catholicism and were determined to move with caution. When Cela Krestos protested, Susenyos agreed to initiate formal conferences on the comparative merits of the two religions. Therefore, on his return to Gorgora, Paez summoned Fr. Antonio de Angelis from

81

Fremona to replace Fernandes at the court of Cela Krestos, who late in 1612 was received into the Roman Church. Others in Gojjam followed, including Azaz-walda Krestos, the courtier, Fequr Eczie, who later led the embassy to Rome, and Za Emmanuel, the Abbot of the monastery of Sellabo. Cela Krestos insisted on proclaiming his new faith publicly, and perhaps rashly, for Emana Krestos had already been threatened with excommunication when he had held discussion with the Jesuits. Soon other officials and friends joined the circle of converts, forming the first nucleus of native Roman Catholics. A third Jesuit residence with a church was then established at Collela, a district of eastern Damot a day's journey from Cela Krestos's court and five days from Gorgora. Like Gorgora but unlike Fremona the new foundation was in the heartland of Ethiopia. In a letter date March 1612 de Angelis wrote that Cela Krestos had insisted on himself helping to lay the foundations of the church and was prepared to meet all the expenses from his own resources.

During these conversations de Angelis had shown Cela Krestos a copy of the *Meditationes in Evangelia* of the Jesuit Geronimo Nadal, published in 1595 with a hundred and fifty-three superb illustrations by the brothers Antoine and Jerome Wierx and numerous other fine Antwerp engravers. Cela Krestos marked his appreciation by donating a sum of gold to have the illustrations coloured; this done, he brought the book to court, where at the request of the Emperor every picture was explained by the Jesuits.*

At court and on the march the Emperor often attended the conferences in which Paez and Fernandes explained the Roman faith. Paez's method was to use the *Hamanot Abau (The Faith of Our Fathers)*, a collection of patristic homilies, apostolic letters, and abstruse discourses on the Trinity and Incarnation, which had authority among the Ethiopians second only to that of the Scrip-

---

* It might be shown that the engravings in Nadal's book introduced new elements into Ethiopian painting. For at least two centuries it had been the custom for monks and priests to insert coloured plates into their sacred books to make more vived the stories of the Bible. Certainly, from about the time of Susenyos, Western inconographic types became common in the decoration of new churches: the Virgin Mary was shown as a delicate maiden in the manner of the Flemish engravers instead of the traditional 'strong woman who is capable of leading the Ethiopian people, protecting them and punishing their enemies'. Cf. Ullendorff, *The Ethiopians*, 168.

tures. Although monophysite in tenor, it contained numerous passages in harmony with Roman teaching with which Paez was able to support his position. Fernandes, the more professional theologian, elucidated difficult texts of Scripture with the aid of Maldonado, the brilliant and popular Jesuit scholar whose lectures at Paris drew such crowds that he was forced to move from the halls of Clermont College to open fields.

There were occasions also when Paez used the same authority. Sitting one day in his tent with Bella Krestos, he was visited by Cela Krestos and some monks who were in the Emperor's camp. First Paez read a passage from Maldonado on a certain text of the New Testament, then asked one of the monks to read their own venerated commentator, one Feragius, on the same text. The two princes, finding Maldonado greatly superior, asked for his books to be translated. Fr. de Angelis was put to the task immediately and with the help of some *dabtara* and Cela Krestos himself had completed the commentaries on the four gospels by the end of 1613. The Emperor and his entourage esteemed particularly Maldonado's exegesis of the Passion narratives and summoned all at court to hear it read, for it seemed to present an authoritative explanation of the true being of Christ, the great issue dividing the Church of Ethiopia from Rome; by contrast their own commentaries were too confused to give any clear guidance. Soon several other books had been made available in translation: the most popular was a work on the creation of the world in six days with added material on the nature of the globe, illustrating God's handiwork; another was a compilation of texts from Greek and Latin Fathers on the Councils of the Church and, almost of necessity, Cardinal Bellarmine on *Christian Doctrine*. To these Fernandes added his own commentary on the Apocalypse. But the literary work of the Jesuits was not directed exclusively to the clergy and court; there were translations made of the psalms and canticles for general use – and, as has been pointed out,* while the Jesuits could not achieve much in their time, they did at least show that Amharic as well as Ge'ez could be used as a literary language.

At both the court and Collela the Jesuits found that the most concerted opposition to their presentation of Roman doctrine came from the monks, who with few exceptions had little or no learning. Drawn often from among unwed deacons and widowed priests,

* Ullendorff, *The Ethiopians*, 150.

they had received no theological education: not even the ability to read was demanded before they were accepted by the superiors of monasterires who had the power to confer on them the status of monks. Although they had no specific duties, their vocation was nevertheless held in esteem, for frequently there were men of genuine holiness among them. For this reason they exercised much greater influence than the ordinary clergy over the people, who listened to the harangues and prophesies by which they generated widespread alarm and fears. In their ignorance the great majority of priests clung blindly to their prejudices, fearful of opening their minds to new influences. Their stubbornness was unassailable as both Paez and the Emperor were to discover.

The first monks had entered the country from Eygpt in the time of St Frumentius in the fourth century and had been followed by others a hundred years later. According to tradition St Takla Haimanot, an Ethiopian, had in the sixth century written rules for these monks, which obliged them to fast every day until three in the afternoon. They said or sang the canonical hours and like the primitive Irish monks were much given to the practice of severe penances, such as standing for hours in cold water in the middle of winter. Many lives were written of St Takla Haimanot, full of miracles, apparitions and extraordinary phenomena. He had led several pilgrimages to Jerusalem and was responsible for the spread and early fervour of Ethiopian monasticism. His family of monks had its mother house at Debra Libanos, later moving to Begameder during the Galla invasions. Another family established by St Eustathius, a fourth-century Egyptian, had its centre at Debra Damo in Tigre but remained comparatively small. After some time in Ethiopia, Eustathius had left for Armenia where he became a missionary.

These two groups differed over the precise substance that formed the physical body of Christ, though both held a monophysite position. The Eustathians maintained the curious view that though Christ was God his body was formed of a substance totally different from that of other human beings. The followers of St Takla held a less esoteric view, but believed that the Son proceeded only from the Father. From the writings of the Jesuits it would seem that very few monks could explain adequately the theological niceties of their tradititional family views. Unlike the Western monks, there had never been a revival among them form the days of their first foundation. Usually they were distinguished from other Ethiopians only

84

From *The Miracles of St George* (British Library, Oriental 713). The lower figure is fishing from a *tankua* on Lake Tana. The two surmounting horsemen are St George and St Mehnam

Children of an Amhara noble

Galla girl at Harar

Monks of a mountain monastery performing a dance

Nativity scene illustrating the influence of Jesuits on Ethiopian art
(British Library, Oriental 510)

Remains of the church built by Pedro Paez, 1619-1621

Above: A priest at
the springs of the Blue
Nile (Colonel R. E.
Cheesman. By courtesy
of the Royal Geograph-
ical Society)

Right: Tisisat Falls at
half-high flood from the
left bank (Colonel R. E.
Cheesman. By courtesy
of the Royal Geograph-
ical Society)

Above: The gorge of the
Blue Nile

Right: On the way from
Tigre to Lake Tana

Reception of the Patriarch Mendes by the Emperor Susenyos, from
Voyage Historique d'Abissinie by Jeronimo Lobo, Paris 1728

by their dress. Both families wore long white garments surmounted by black cowls. Some who lived luxuriously, the 'wordly ones', were found at court; others who professed poverty were clothed in leather in winter and in undyed linen in summer. The nuns acknowledged the same two monks as their founders and formed their own communities in the neighbourhood of the monasteries. Only the better foundations provided any education for their aspirants. The majority held blindly and by rote to their traditional beliefs. It was these who wanted to 'assign to the flames Maldondo on the Four Gospels, Toledo on the Romans and Pedro Ribadeneira on the Hebrews, since they totally demolished their arguments'.*

Never far from the Emperor's camp, the Abuna Simon determined to defend his position by excommunicating all who held that there were two natures in Christ. For a time he was restrained by Bella Krestos, the Emperor's half-brother, who had professed himself a Roman Catholic about the same time as Cela Krestos, and was highly regarded for his sharp intellect, theological learning and skill as a military tactician. During one heated exchange between him and the Abuna Simon, the Emperor broke in, called for calm and closed the conference. He declared that the Ethiopian books came down on the side of two natures in the one Person, which henceforth must be accepted as sound and solid doctrine.

Simon was silent. With the backing of angry traditionalists he later sought an audience of Susenyos. Without any theological argument on his side, his plea was that the Coptic Church and Ethiopia were indissolubly wedded: it was a bond the Jesuits were seeking to break, and they should therefore be expelled. Susenyos shrugged his shoulders in scorn, pointing out that all the rulers in the country were now showing their appreciation of the Fathers, and that in Za Dengel's time they had been given permission to instruct all who wished to become Roman Catholics.

Simon however, denied that such permission had ever been granted. Later at court, with a circle of monks supporting him, he charged the Jesuits with seducing his subjects from the allegiance they owed him personally. The Portuguese, he complained, had

---

* Cardinal Francisco Toledo (1532-96), an eminent Jesuit professor of the Roman College, was considered one of the most learned men of his age; Pedro de Ribadeneira (1526-1611), a brilliant writer whose works are rated Castilian classics.

entered the country as soldiers; since they came without wives, they had married Ethiopian women and converted them to Roman Catholicism. This, of course, was true, but the Jesuits replied that it was not good for husband and wife to be of different religions, and that in any case this had been the practice now for some seventy years without any objection being raised. The Abuna Simon was not satisfied. He argued that many European Catholics under the jurisdiction of the Pope and living in Jerusalem or Memphis did not attempt to convert their wives. To this the Jesuits retorted that in Ethiopia the case was different because the wives taken by the Portuguese were already Christian.

The Emperor was absent from this last conference but on his return to court came down on the side of the Jesuits; he sent them messengers reaffirming their freedom to preach and to receive converts. Simon could not contain his rage. For fear that he might stir up a rebellion, Paez proposed a compromise: only those wives should become Romans who insisted on it. Unsatisfied with this, Simon at a solemn celebration of Mass pronounced an awesome excommunication in the name of the apostles Peter and Paul against anyone who so much as dared greet the Fathers even from the entrance to their houses. Bella Krestos showed what he thought of this by visiting the Fathers at Gorgora while Susenyos sent a messenger bidding them be of good heart and to ignore the excommunication. He made his theological position clear when a monk offered him a hymn of his own composition. When Cela Krestos was given it for censorship he detected in the prologue certain phrases that could be taken to question the two natures of Christ. The monk was reproved by the Emperor, who after the lines had been amended gave it to his choir master to be set to music.

Since any form of excommunication was dreaded by the Ethiopians the Abuna Simon could not have put himself in more complete and inflexible opposition to the Emperor. The formula he used made it total, absolute and, in the estimation of people, divinely endorsed. 'There is no nation,' wrote one of the Fathers, 'where excommunication carries greater terrors than among the Abyssinians, which puts it in the power of the priests to abuse the religious temper of the people . . . by excommunicating them, as they often do, for the least trifle in which their interest is concerned.'

Susenyos had little regard for Simon. As the nominee of Cairo, the Abuna represented a hostile as well as an alien people; he had, in fact, always to be an Egyptian according to an apocryphal canon of the Council of Nicaea (325), which was observed until recently. Nor, as Paez noted, could he even be an Ethiopian monk from Jerusalem. Nevertheless he exercised unquestioned and unlimited authority in a country where as a foreigner he was usually unfamiliar with the language, culture and revered customs of the people.* He alone could anoint and crown the Emperor, confer sacred orders and dispense from vows. However, apart from the occasions when he was used as a tool by others, he seldom played an important part in ecclesiastical affairs. The routine administration of the Church was left to the *echage*, who in practice had more power than the Abuna: he governed through provincial deputies, presented candidates for ordination and settled disputes over the liturgy. In the Emperor's estimation the life of the Abuna Simon compared unfavourably with that of the Jesuits, who appeared dedicated men and, unlike Simon, did not amass personal wealth.

In addition to the dues he received for ordination, the Abuna held three or four large estates as *gult*, the system that allowed him to retain the tribute normally paid to the Emperor. His lands in Tigre alone were said to yield four to five hundred *patacas†* in gold, while those in Dambea were sufficient to provide for his household. Further lands in Gojjam, however, were of less value because they were subject to frequent attacks by the Galla. The views of the Jesuits on the Abunas are summarized by one of them who wrote: 'Several Fathers of the Society affirm that they knew three or four Abunas, none of whom they ever heard teach or preach; and they seem to be of the number of those of whom the prophet Isaiah says, "They are all dumb dogs, they cannot bark." ' Francisco Alvares, the chaplain to the first embassy who relates in minute detail everything he witnessed, does not mention that he ever heard the Abuna Mark preach, but he did see him confer orders which was his principal work. On that occasion he asked those who had been married

* In 1926 a petition was made to Alexandria for a native prelate and in 1929 a compromise was reached by which, though still an Egyptian, the Abuna was assisted by four native bishops. In 1948 he was chosen for the first time from an Ethiopian monastery, and after approval by the Negus was consecrated by the Egyptian Patriarch. Finally, in January 1959, the Ethiopian Church became totally independent of Egypt.

† An old Castilian silver coin worth a drime of gold.

twice not to receive them, but he accepted candidates who were blind, lame and halt.

The Abuna Simon was in a particularly unenviable position. When his predecessor Peter was killed in a battle he had been sent from Alexandria without being asked for by the Emperor, who already before his coronation had opened negotiations for a Patriarch from Rome – a move that was checked by both Paez and the Viceroy on the ground that it was premature. All the same Simon had cause to loathe the Jesuits; they on their side had nothing good to say of him. To them Simon was a man reared *inter scelera Turcarum* in Memphis, and was steeped in their unspeakable morals. What else could be expected of a man who had lived among the fiercest enemies of Christianity? They said he was no shepherd, that he never kept watch over his flock, gave them no spiritual fodder and, instead of directing them to the study of Scripture, 'diverted them to marshy and pest-ridden waters', setting an example of licentious conduct. It was said that he lived in open adultery with the wife of an Egyptian domiciled in the country and kept a large harem of native girls. When one of these gave birth to a child he had it exposed to the hyenas to devour.

Although it was not the custom in for the people to confess their individual sins, the Abuna Simon was known sometimes to practise a peculiar rite of absolution which is recorded by Alvares. On the occasions when he would appear among the people so that they could approach him for indulgences, penitents would also come to him to confess their sins in public in the belief that they thus obtained a fuller pardon. They would mention one or two sins that in the mind of the faithful were considered heinous. This done, Simon stood up and with his staff gave the penitent three or four good strokes, saying to him, 'Have you done so and so? Do you not fear God? Go and receive thirty or forty lashes.' Then the Mazarines, or officers attending the Abuna, would begin to whip the penitent with the thongs they carried for keeping the people at a distance. The flogging was always severe, but sometimes when the poor man had received six or seven lashes the company would intercede for him. 'After this unsavoury absolution the penitent withdrew, glad with all his heart to be delivered from the Abuna's staff and the throngs of the Mazarines.'

Over these simple people the Abuna Simon exercised an influence second only to that of the Emperor. He was received everywhere with great honour and ceremony. His monopoly of conferring Orders was a subject that had a professional interest for Paez, for in the event of reunion the question of their validity could not be brushed aside. Several times Paez returned to the problem in his letters, and in his *History* he went into the question in detail. Since candidates were always numerous, they were ordained in large groups together. Paez watched an ordination but was never permitted to see the text of the Ordinal: the words of the formula were in a kind of Arabic he did not understand. When Cela Krestos asked on his behalf to be shown the book, he was refused. Paez therefore withheld his judgement, though from his description of the service it is clear that he had doubts about their validity.

The crowds of ordinands would assemble outside a church or tent, for they could never be contained inside any building. They usually sat on the grass in three rows and were counted so as to ascertain how many *pedras* or bars of salt, which were accepted currency everywhere, had to be collected as tax. Paez explains that salt was as useful as gold but he doubted the story that it was carried as far west as Monomotapa and the Congo. Found on the Dankal border, its value varied in proportion to the distance it was conveyed over the mountains by donkey or mule. The Jesuit Almeida found it pitiful to 'see the roads from Tigre to Dambea all constantly full of people in caravans of a thousand servers (as they call men who carry it) and five hundred donkeys loaded with these bars, so great that they are crushed by their burdens'. Travelling south the caravans were lightened, as at every frontier post dues were exacted in *pedras*. The salt became rarer still as the animals, losing their foothold on the narrow mountain passes, fell headlong down the precipices.

After the prelate had calculated the *pedras* due to him, the ceremony of ordination proceeded. Each candidate was then marked with a cross in ink near the wrist on the right hand, after which the Abuna, seated at the entrance to his tent, read a text and all to be ordained came up in turn to receive his Order. The ceremony was the same for all Orders with the exception of the priesthood, which was conferred during the celebration of Mass. Only for this was there any examination. In theory the ordinand was required to pass a test in reading. The passages demanded were always the same, the beginning of St John's Gospel and the second and twenty-third chapters of the Acts of the Apostles. To deceive the examiners the candidates formed themselves into groups according to the districts where they lived, then from each group one candidate who could read well answered the call to represent the rest, who were then approved without further probing. 'I asked one of the better educated monks,' wrote Paez, 'whether the candidates were examined on any points of Scripture and theology. The monk answered with a smile. "Neither the examiner nor the Abuna knows any. How can they ask any questions? The examination is only for reading." '

The system was hardly calculated to produce an educated clergy. Nevertheless priests enjoyed great prestige among the people as the privileged ministers of the sacred mysteries. Apart from the duty of offering Mass for the people, their life differed little from that of the peasants: like them, they ploughed, harvested and did business in the market. Generally they were not noted for their strict moral conduct. As Paez discovered, they were frequently drunk, devious and quarrelsome. All the same, through the influence they exercised locally they could turn the nation against the sovereign, who would be ill-advised to incur their hostility indefinitely. Short of using violent methods, such as flogging or imprisonment, the Emperor could discipline them, at least for short periods, by refusing them benefices. To maintain their numbers when it seemed likely that the country would be deprived of an Abuna for a long period, children were often ordained to bridge the gap.

The Abuna Simon's influence at court declined daily. Paez drew closer to Susenyos and more intimate with him. Either on his own initiative or at the Emperor's request Paez had sent to Goa for a signet ring to be made there and despatched with all haste. When it came within a year, the Emperor was delighted with the gift: it depicted the Lion of Judah wearing the imperial crown of Ethiopia, finely engraved by the best craftsmen in Goa. He said that he treasured it 'more than the five horses recently given him by the ruler of Agame', a district to the east of Aksum. Susenyos could hardly have used words of greater appreciation. Although mules were more useful in the mountainous regions, horses were prized for their speed in battle to the degree that many famous Ethiopian warriors were known by their horse's name, which was used also as a war cry by their foot soldiers when they charged the enemy. Together with other gifts, Paez gave the Emperor a jug with a long narrow spout and some finely carved statues, which he returned to the Jesuits for their church at Gorgora.

The appreciation shown by the Emperor for the signet ring

encouraged Paez to demonstrate what the Portuguese could do by way of domestic building; or, as he put it, to show the Ethiopians that all the Fathers had said about the palaces and monasteries in Europe was not fictitious, as they were inclined to believe. In spite of the turmoil of war, Paez now planned a noble palace unlike anything yet seen in Ethiopia. Work was begun in May 1614 on a site where there was good white stone. Paez trained his own work crew. He first showed them how to make hammers, mallets, chisels and other tools he needed, then how to hew and square the stone, and finally he instructed joiners and carpenters. He lacked lime and could find no substitute for it. Instead he used a binding type of clay. With this he was able to raise large and strong walls that he faced both inside and outside with squared stone; all was 'so well wrought and joined that the building when finished might serve any prince in Europe for a country house'. The main hall measured fifty feet by fifteen; and on the same floor he made a square bedchamber with a spacious staircase in the centre. On the floor above was a second staircase that led on to a flat roof surrounded with a parapet. Here was a little room like a closet which gave the Emperor a distant view over the lake and from which 'he saw all at hand come in and out, without himself being discovered'. To the south-west the skyline was broken by Debra Semona in Gojjam; due south, the peak of Amadir, 12,000 feet, could be seen seventy miles away, and to the south-west Mount Gana in Begameder, 14,000 feet, seventy-five miles from Gorgora.

People came far to look at the palace. What surprised them most was the upper floor: they had no word to describe it and called it *babet laybet* or a house upon a house. On the door of the stairs leading to the flat roof Paez made a spring lock, which the Emperor asked to be altered because he did not wish to bothered with a key. Paez objected. 'Your Majesty may have occasion to use it,' he said, perhaps prophetically, for some time later three conspirators – Julius, the Governor of Tigre, with the Master of the Palace and Yamana Krestos, the Emperor's brother sought an audience of Susenyos with the intention of assassinating him. Warned of their intentions, the Emperor rose sedately from his chair and took the visitors to the door leading to the roof. Slipping through it, he slammed it in their face. The conspirators, realizing that they had been discovered, fled.

The flat roof was itself an innovation, for it was found only in the

91

Turkish-occupied parts of Tigre and at Debaroa. The palace dominated the imperial camp and the homes of the grandees, which consisted usually of six or eight small thatched houses enclosed within a wall of rock or stone surmounted by thorn scrub woven into it. Even the Jesuit Almeida, who saw the palace five or six years after its completion, was impressed; he called it:

> a wonder in that country and something that had never been seen or even imagined, and it was such as would have value and be reckoned a handsome building anywhere. It stands inside two very wide and long enclosures in a situation dominating all the rest and is therefore visible a long way off. It has halls and rooms on the ground floor and the upper floor, very well proportioned, and terraces from which can be seen not only the camp and the whole of Dancaz, but even distant places in all directions.

After Susenyos's reign the palace was replaced by the new buildings in the first static capital of Ethiopia at Gondar, and was no longer occupied. Probably the earthquake that destroyed the greater part of Gondar fifty miles away in 1704 also threw down most of the roofing of Paez's palace. An English traveller, R. E. Cheesman, visiting the ruins in 1930, was as impressed as Paez's contemporaries had been. He wrote:

> we passed into a very large courtyard with a fish-pool or rain water tank inside the walls and a stone gutter spout draining into it from the roof. Rooms are built along the outside wall. The keyed arches all round show skilled workmanship and many are still standing. On the east side of the court is a high wall of rock, each block of which is shaped, and this formed the main support of the great banquet hall. The wall is double and broad enough to carry a stone stairway up its interior. We ascended this and stood on the parapet on the top, some seventy feet above the ground. We did not find the door with the spring lock mentioned in Paez's story.
>
> On the west of the wall are beam rests that supported the floor of a second storey, of which there is no sign today. The eastern part of the main wall forms the side of a magnificently conceived banquet hall, this wall and part of the arched span of the roof at the south end being all that remains to show the design. The wall is decorated throughout its length by a row of false windows several feet in diameter, carved in rock in rose pattern, with a row of inverted shell pattern carvings. Considering their long exposure to the weather they are in excellent condition. All the stone pillars are carved in an infinite variety of patterns.*

* Cheesman, *Lake Tana and the Blue Nile*, 208.

92

The residence at Gorgora replaced Fremona in importance, for it was close to the now permanent camp of the Emperor at Dancaz. The first house and church were no more than the simple round huts of the kind that Paez found at Fremona on his arrival there in 1603. By 1610 the school was well established. A report two years later speaks of a church in Enarya, situated on an island, an impressive building of which the Abuna was forced to admit he had not seen the like in Memphis. From the foundations to its completion the work was directed by the Jesuits themselves. The Emperor donated to the Fathers fifty ounces of gold for their support, but they gave most of it to war widows and the poor.

In the summer of that year Susenyos, about to leave Dancaz with his army, was told of a crib erected by the Fathers at Gorgora and called to visit it. He asked Paez to have it removed to another church nearer the camp where crowds came to see it. There was such excitement and uproar over it that the monks had to use their scourges to control the crowds. The construction of a crib was yet another means used by Paez to attract people to the Roman Church. During the years of his captivity in San'â he would have heard from Monserrate how at Agra the crib had become an important feature of the mission; it had been built there each year by skilled craftsmen under the direction of the Fathers. Recently Jeronimo Xavier had written to tell him how he would sit by the crib and count sometimes fourteen thousand, sometimes more, visitors a day, Christians, Muslims and Hindus to whom he would explain what it meant.

Susenyos had delayed his reply to Pope Paul V. The ships sailing from Goa had already left when his letter arrived; and since he wanted a consensus at court before making an approach to Rome, he waited until early 1613 before writing. By then the conferences had shown a majority around the Emperor in favour of closer ties with the West. Binding the Jesuits and his brother Cela Krestos to secrecy he told them he had taken an oath to become a Catholic and was ready to receive a Patriarch appointed by the Pope. Unable to commit this to writing for fear that secrecy would be breached, as had happened when Za Dengel wrote to Rome in June 1604, he decided to send an oral message through an ambassador.

The envoy chosen was Fecur Eczie, a man of courage and intelligence, the convert to Catholicism who had helped Fr. de Angelis with his translation of Maldonado. The Emperor was anxious for one of the Jesuits to accompany him. When Paez offered to go, Susenyos protested that he was needed at court. However, the

Emperor promised to assist in every possible way whoever might be sent. 'I shall write to the King of Enarya,' he declared, 'so that the Father chosen as envoy can reach the port of Melinde safely with his military escort.'

The choice fell on Fernandes who, after Paez, was closest to the Emperor and the court. In addition to the letters he was to write, Susenyos entrusted him with private messages for the Pope. Cela Krestos was deputed to make all the arrangements for the embassy.

Five letters in all were drawn up: three written by the Emperor – to the Pope, to Philip III of Spain and to the Viceroy of the Indies – and with them two from Cela Krestos, to the Pope again and to the King. Susenyos explained in his letter to the Pope that because of the monsoons the Portuguese ships had already left that year; so he had decided to despatch the embassy 'by another road which we hope God will keep open'. He added that the Fathers of the Society had brought him to an understanding of the true faith of the blessed St Peter. 'We have determined,' he concluded, 'to embrace that faith and to render obedience to your Holiness as to the head of the univesal Church, and henceforth to govern ourselves by your Patriarch.' For this he needed immediate help from Don Felipe, 'now at this present time, and in your blissful reign', so that 'so good an opportunity may not be lost'. The letter was dated 31 January 1613 in 'our court in Dambea'.

The letter to Philip III was equally pressing but more explicit. It reiterated his earlier request for troops 'to enable us to render publicly this obedience to the See of Peter and to receive a Patriarch from there'. At least a thousand Portuguese were needed: 'When they come, they must take the port of Massawa in the strait of the Red Sea, and I shall give them the coast lands and help them to hold them; for the rest we refer you to the Father and to our ambassador.'

In his letter to the Viceroy, Susenyos gave his detailed plans for the deployment of the Portuguese troops: five hundred were required to take the port of Massawa and the coastal lands and to hold them against reoccupation, and another thousand to form a regular force in the field with the Emperor, along with their armourers and construction workers. For the rest he again referred the Viceroy to his ambassador and to Fr. Fernandes.

Paez still did not press Susenyos to declare himself a convert to Rome. Since reaching Massawa in 1603 he had managed to keep up an exchange of letters with Jeronimo Xavier, whose missionary approach at the court of Akbar was similar to his own at Dancaz. They shared the hope that the two great Emperors, each in his own time, would accept the Roman faith along with all their subject people. The year 1613, which saw the despatch of Susenyos's envoys to Europe, held out almost unbelievable expectations of conversion in all four great empires in which the small band of Jesuit missionaries were at work; for both China, thanks to Ricci, and Japan, under the direction of Valignano, also seemed on the verge of accepting Roman Catholicism as the faith of their nations.

In a letter he had received from Xavier about this time, Paez heard that his friend had been teaching Portuguese to the three young sons of Akbar's deceased brother and had also instructed them in Christian doctrine. When the day of their baptism arrived, the three boys, dressed in Portuguese ruffs, came to church in a procession of elephants adorned in crimson velvet with gold trimmings. They removed their hats on entering and bowed in the Portuguese manner. Asked in front of the congregation whether they wished to become Catholics the three princes, aged seven, eight and nine, declared that they knew well what they were doing, and were then baptized taking the names of Philip, Charles and Henry. It was a day of great rejoicing for, until a short time before the christening, the Mogul Emperor had been hostile to the Jesuits. Now he welcomed the boys on their return to the palace and gave each of them several gold coins, which they in turn offered to the priests. Lessons were then continued and a fourth nephew of Akbar's joined the class and was duly led to church in a procession of elephants accompanied by musicians and gentlemen of the court.

Before Susenyos's envoy left Dancaz he was received in a formal audience along with Cela Krestos and Fernandes. Paez was present. 'Go,' said the Emperor, 'with the blessing of God who by no uncertain signs has indicated that I should embrace the true faith.' Speaking of the Abuna Simon and his circle he rejoiced in the failure of their efforts to deflect his affection from the Fathers. 'I want to commit the administration of the Church to the Pope,' he said, 'and to venerate the Patriarch he shall send to correct our errors.' Then he swore by the Cross of Christ that he would strive to unite his Church with Rome. This was the gravest of oaths.

Cela Krestos was in favour of travelling by the way of Massawa, but Susenyos was confident that providence would see his ambassador safe through Enarya to Melinde. Paez also questioned the wis-

95

dom of choosing this route. In fact he was astonished that it should have been considered at all, for it meant travelling from Dambea, where the Emperor was encamped on the north side of Tana, through Gojjam, over the Blue Nile, then across the southern kingdoms, which owed little more than nominal allegiance to the empire, and beyond their frontiers to Melinde, some hundred miles north of Mombasa. In a direct line it was a journey of one thousand two hundred miles, largely through territory inhabited, as Paez wrote, by 'Moors, Turks, Cafres and other barbarous nations'. But Susenyos was insistent that this route, which the early Portuguese had failed to find, should now be attempted.

On leaving, Fernandes was embraced by the Emperor. Without mishap the party reached Collela, where they were welcomed by Fr. Antonio de Angelis. The Emperor had given them two hundred pieces of gold to cover their expenses. From Collela they set out for Melinde on 25 March 1613.

6

Fernandes's attempt to reach Melinde, the seaport on the African east coast where the fleet from India called on its way to Lisbon, is one of the most remarkable chapters in the history of early African exploration.

From Collela the ambassador and Fernandes went to Wambarma, a district between the rivers Zingini and Fatam, where Cela Krestos was encamped. The Viceroy kept them there until he had procured for them guides from the heathen tribes through whose territory they were to pass on the first part of their journey.* Before Fernandes left, Cela Krestos addressed him 'with great fervour,' Almeida writes,

> and in the spirit one might have expected from a Superior of the Society when sending a subordinate on a laborious and difficult mission. He represented to him the importance of the business with which he was entrusted and the difficulties the devil would raise to prevent him from attaining the desired end. . . . He reminded him that amid the greatest toils and dangers he should put his trust in God, being certain and sure that the Lord would not fail to help him, since he had exposed himself to them for His love and since the entire enterprise was wholly His. He especially urged him to try to conclude the business with the greatest possible speed and despatch, so that their intentions could be put into effect during the Emperor's lifetime; if he should die before him, all would be in vain and the cost and trouble of the journey would be wasted.

His eyes filling with tears, Cela Krestos attempted to kiss Fer-

* The following pages are based on Almeida's account of Fernandes's journey, translated and edited by C. F. Beckingham and G. W. B. Huntingford in *Some Records of Ethiopia 1593-1646*.

nandes's feet; frustrated in this, he begged the Jesuit to kneel at the Pope's feet and kiss them on his behalf and, if possible, bring back a small thread of his clothing that he could preserve as a relic. He asked Fernandes to make known to the Holy Father that he had no greater desire than to visit Rome and the courts of Portugal.

On 15 April 1613 the party left Wambarma with an escort of forty men all 'armed with darts and targets' and pushed westward. After three days they were held up by a heathen tribe of Galla called Gonga before they had even got as far as the Nile. When it became known that they had summoned help from Cela Krestos they were allowed to continue. Three days later they struck the Blue Nile at a place Fernandes calls Mina, thought by cartographers to have been Mabil, where a caravan route went direct to Sarka, the capital of Enarya. Five days was a long time to take over such a short distance, but it can be explained by either the weather or the terrain or the incompetence of their guides. Here a crossing was negotiated on a 'float of sticks tied together with some gourds or calabashes to support it', pulled and pushed by swimmers. Since the float could not hold more than a small amount of baggage and a few persons, the crossing took an entire day.

From the Nile they travelled south. After another seven days they reached the northern frontier of Enarya at a place called Ganca; this is not found on modern maps but occurs in chronicles in the phrase 'the frontiers of Enarya and Ganqua'. Here they encountered another tribe of Galla who attempted to rob them but were bought off with pieces of muslin and bars of salt. When three days later they met a large caravan coming north from Enarya and enquired about conditions on the route, they were told that such a small party as theirs was certain to be overwhelmed by brigands. Hearing this some traders travelling with them turned back, but a man from the northbound caravan was persuaded to join them and undertook to guide them by devious tracks to escape likely ambushes. After further adventures they reached the court of Benero, the King of Enarya, a country that had recently adopted Christianity and formed part of the Ethiopian Empire. Fernandes calls the inhabitants 'the best people of Ethiopia, as the Abyssinians themselves admit. They are well shaped, their lips are thin, their noses sharp, their colour not very black' – a description totally inapplicable to the present-day inhabitants of the country still known as Enarya. 'Their land yields plenty of grain,' Fernandes continues, 'and feeds an

98

abundance of cattle'; their gold was dealt by weight, and for coins they beat out flat light pieces of iron two fingers broad and three in length.

When word reached Susenyos of the safe arrival of the embassy in Enarya he was convinced more than before that he was right in his choice of route. In a letter that reached Paez at Fremona on 2 June he mentioned Fernandes's arrival there. Paez, however, was not so confident because about that time the Galla, now active again in the north, had killed many travellers on the road between Tana and Massawa.

Fernandes was received with kindness by King Benero, but also with some reservation. This was due to an Ethiopian missionary at his court, who presumed that Fernandes proposed to stay there, 'so depriving him of the office of chaplain and vicar-general of the Abuna Simon in the country, and of the income he collected which was not small'.

Susenyos, when writing to Paez, who was then at Fremona, was unaware that Fernandes had been compelled by Benero to abandon the planned route to Melinde. Rightly suspecting that the purpose of the embassy was to seek Portuguese military assistance, the King was afraid that, if this line of communication to the coast was opened up, the Portuguese would enter that way and make themselves masters of his kingdom. Benero was only loosely the vassal of the Emperor; he had already driven out the Galla and now he had no intention of becoming a subject of the Portuguese. Instead of helping the party on their journey south-east towards Melinde, the king insisted on their continuing eastward through Bali, a kingdom that bordered on Adal. This would have brought them out on the coast in the area of Cape Guardafui, but only after they had crossed the desert of Ogaden and passed through Somaliland. The king knew well that no Portuguese or Ethiopian embassy would be given safe conduct through all this Muslim-held territory.

Fernandes protested unavailingly. With a small escort provided by Benero he set out through what was then the southern limits of the empire, a region not again described by a European traveller before the nineteenth century. On this part of their way they travelled only by night; during the day they hid in woods for fear of marauding Galla, knowing that if they were caught they would be forced to drink boiling water. Luck was with them. Chased by a group of Galla they escaped across the river Omo or, as Fernandes calls it, the Gibe, which rises in the central highlands south of Addis Ababa and takes a south-westerly course to empty into Lake Rudolph in Kenya, draining a populous country of Galla settlements. At this point it flowed between precipices of upright rock – 'to look down on it was to look into hell'. The planks that the guides laid across from one rock to another sagged as if they were green twigs when a foot was placed on them. The crossing was perilous enough, but their dread of the Galla was even greater.

On the further bank they entered the small kingdom of Gingero, the modern Janjero, in south-west central Ethiopia, where they were abandoned by their escort. Here they waited eight days for permission to go to court, for the local king was busy with his magicians offering sacrifices. When they were finally received they found the potentate sitting on a sort of railed tower about eighteen feet high. All the nobles clustered round him. He looked 'not unlike a monkey on a block'. He was wearing a white Indian silk garment, and he himself was as black as coal. Fernandes's conversation with him was carried on through an interpreter who had first to kiss the tips of the king's fingers every time he started a new sentence, then fall down and kiss the ground before going to Fernandes who stood some distance away. The answer was delivered with the same ritual.

The king promised the party assistance. Presents were exchanged. The king's gift to the Jesuit was a young attractive female slave, which he graciously exchanged for a male slave and a mule.

From Gingero the embassy passed into the kingdom of Kambatta, south of Addis Ababa and to the west of a chain of lakes running from Lake Zwai, the largest and most northerly of the south Ethiopian lakes, to Lake Rudolph. The frontier here was a river, probably a branch of the Omo, where they again suffered anguish in getting across. This time the guides contrived a method that was new to Fernandes. Killing a cow, they made a great sack of its hide into which they put their baggage. Then blowing strongly, they filled it with air like a bladder, so that it could serve as a boat. They then took two poles and fastened them to the blown-up hide. Two men on each side hung on to these poles, holding the hide steady. If one person moved all were in danger of plunging into the stream. The boat was guided by a good swimmer pulling a rope fastened to the hide, while two others swam behind thrusting it forward.

No sooner were they across than they were attacked by natives from the neighbouring kingdom of Gurage. Although the party could muster now only seventeen armed men, it beat off the assailants for the loss of a kinsman of the ambassador, killed by a poisoned arrow. Hamelmal, the ruler of Kambatta, like the King of Enarya, was a vassal of Susenyos; like him also, he suspected that the true purpose of the mission was to bring in the Portuguese. Every obstacle was now put in its way.

What made things worse for Fernandes was that his arrival coincided with that of Susenyos's representative, whose name is given as Manker. He had come to collect tribute due to the Emperor. That at least was the pretext for his presence, but in fact he had been despatched by the anti-Jesuit faction at court to harry the embassy and block its further progress.

This Manker asserted that the envoys had come without the Emperor's permission and that their real purpose was not religious, but military:

> They were to bring in foreign troops in order to force them to change their religion, bartering the faith of their fathers and grandfathers for that of Rome . . . He was not satisfied with persuading only Hamelmal of this. He laboured to convince all the people of that country and the neighbouring districts, Galla, Moors and Christians. He instilled great fear into them, reminding them that when the Moor Grañ had conquered almost the whole of Ethiopia, a few Portuguese had been enough to free it from his hands, because they were very brave, and fought with muskets and bombards that struck terror into everyone and killed from a long way off.

Hamelmal, hearing this, sent messengers to Susenyos and held the party prisoner until its *bona fides* was established.

The first messengers, with the connivance of Manker, spent three months at a village just a week's journey away, then returned saying they had been held prisoners there and had been unable to make further progress. Others were sent. When these eventually reached the imperial court Susenyos was angered that his embassy to the Pope should have been held up through the machinations of a man belonging to the Abuna Simon's faction. He first considered sending a punitive expedition against Kambatta; prevented by sheer distance, he despatched letters to Hamelmal commanding him to do everything possible to secure for Fernandes and the ambassador

> the favour of neighbouring kings and princes so that they should all grant them free and open passage through their countries. With this

101

object he sent rich *cabayas* to Hamelmal and also to a Moor who governed a country near there called Alaba, the Moor himself being called Alico; he was the first person through whose country the Father and ambassador had to go when they left Hamelmal's principality.

Fernandes had now been travelling for fourteen months. The day before the Ides of April (12 April 1614), writes the author of the annual Jesuit report, 'the king of Kambatta, on reading the letter from the Emperor, freed Fernandes from chains but detained him in the kingdom for some time, allowing him to leave only at the end of June for Alaba, the small state south-west of Lake Shala, three days' journey away'.

Manker had prevented Fernandes's earlier departure in order to plot with the Moorish governor of Alaba to block any further progress of the embassy. On arriving at Alaba, Fernandes and all with him were immediately arrested, their goods, money and mules were seized and even their clothes taken from them. Fernandes slept on the ground, hungry and cold. For twelve days, weakened now by his imprisonment, he remained close to death. During this time he made pretence of enjoying tobacco and asked a friendly Moor for fire to light a pipe. He was given a flame and with it secretly burned all the letters he was carrying, 'to prevent being set on fire himself', as he later wrote to Susenyos.

While the party was in prison Manker discussed with Alico whether all of them should be killed. In the end it was agreed that they should be set free but only on condition that they returned to Ethiopia by a route that made it impossible for them to strike for the coast. Three Portuguese were detained by Alico to serve in his wars: two of them were later liberated by Cela Krestos, the third died in captivity.

With a Moorish guide provided by Alico the remainder made their way through Galla-held territory, crossing the Hawash which Fernandez calls the Oaxe. This is the second largest river in Ethiopia, rising a short distance south of Addis and flowing east, then north-east, in the direction of the Red Sea at Djibouti; yet it never reaches the sea, for it either disappears, as Fernandes reported, in the sands of the Somali desert or evaporates under the equatorial sun. On its banks Fernandes saw an encampment of some eight thousand Galla grazing their immense herds. The only European to record an encounter with them here, he is not ashamed to admit his terror of this 'barbarian race': they drink, he said, the blood of cows

102

extracted from their veins with a stylus. 'More like beasts than men, they cultivate no arts, and for the sake of pleasure they kill innocent men like cats.'

At this point a new guide was obtained. They were conducted safely through Shoa, a broad level plain uncut for immense distances by any mountains, then north into Gojjam, rugged and mountainous in most parts, where marching became slower, and back to Collela. There Fernandes wrote to Susenyos to explain the failure of his mission and at the same time profess his readiness to try again. In late September 1614, nineteen months after leaving for Melinde and Rome, Fernandes was back at the Emperor's camp. Manker, meanwhile, believing that he must have been killed, returned to court, where the Emperor at once condemned him to death. Paez says that at the insistence of Fernandes himself the sentence was commuted to banishment on a remote amba. On his way to exile, Manker was murdered by a party of Galla, the very fate he had plotted for the Jesuit.

With the failure of the embassy to reach Melinde the Papacy was deprived of a first-hand account of conditions in Ethiopia. This loss, which was never made good, proved tragic in the course of the next decade.

While Fernandes was away, Susenyos spent two winters in the country of the Agau in an attempt to reduce them to more complete subjection to the empire. Paez accompanied him on these campaigns and got to know the people, who at this time were to be found in two provinces – in Lasta, a wild district of Begameder, and in Agaumdir, a mountainous area in the east of Gojjam, close to the Nile which it encircled. This district was full of woods in which bamboos grew so densely that they formed a natural defence against any hostile assualt. The picture drawn by Paez of these defences is not unlike the trench system of the First World War: he observed how the Agau cut through the bamboos close narrow tracks that became labyrinths. Here in time of war, about a mile from the entrance, they shut themselves in and laid trees across the devious paths. From the *secutes*, as they were called, the Agau shot their arrows. As a further defence they used vast underground caves called *furtatas* that could conceal large numbers of men behind narrow entrances until the enemy had passed. The Agau were good soldiers and had for long maintained their hold on the districts where they had first settled, both against Cafres or African pagans and against the Ethiopian

Emperors, their nominal overlords. Traditionally they regarded war as a lesser evil than peace; war could inflict little damage on them, while peace meant oppression. The only clothing for both men and women was two lengths of cowhide beaten until it became like leather, dyed red and fastened about the waist.

Susenyos pressed them hard and forced them into submission. Then Paez, whom the Agau knew to have influence at court, was approached by them to intercede on their behalf. He was offered many gifts, all of which he refused; the only condition he laid down was that the Agau should receive a Christian missionary in their country. Paez pleaded with Susenyos to be allowed to go himself, since he had joined the Society for this kind of work rather than for a life at court. The Emperor, however, insisted once more that his presence was necessary there but agreed to allow Fr. Antonio de Angelis to take his place. A mission was duly established, but de Angelis at first showed no great affection for the people, who suspected him of being a spy, a sorcerer and a heretic. He was about to be driven out of their country when the Agau's very existence was threatened by an incursion of a neighbouring colony of Galla. In the battles that ensued each seized the other's herds and destroyed the other's dwellings until the Agau won the day; they had the advantage of fighting in their own country and of being able to retire to their *furtatas* when they were temporarily worsted. Moreover, during these years 'they increased extremely, every man being allowed as many wives as he had hundreds of cattle, and it was seldom that the hundreds were required to be completed'.

During these skirmishes de Angelis showed sympathy for the cause of the Agau and established himself in their favour. His preaching among them was the only direct missionary enterprise undertaken by the Jesuits in Paez's time. The districts they occupied had never been effectively evangelized by the established Church, and in so far as Christianity took root there it became a Roman Catholic enclave of the empire. By 1620 de Angelis had mastered their language, built a church and made numerous converts, in spite of the insinuations of the clergy that if they became Roman Catholics they would provoke fresh Galla attacks. When, that same year, the Emperor passed through their country, de Angelis with their chieftains came out to meet him bringing gifts of honey. Fernandes reported these events to Rome in 1620, writing that the Agau were less brown than the Abyssinians, intelligent and docile.

While de Angelis was working among the Agau, Pedro Paez in company with the Emperor visited the source of the Blue Nile. He does not claim to have discovered where the river rose: it was not a subject he even mentioned in any of his long extant letters to his friend Iturén, in which he recounts the events of each year. In his *History* he says he went to the source of the river and he describes what he saw, not as a discovery – although his account is the first ever written by a European – but simply as something that for the sake of completion should be mentioned in the kind of history of the country he was engaged in writing. In Paez's long book on Ethiopia his description of the source of the Blue Nile occupies only four out of 1,128 printed pages and is given in the context of the two rivers that account for the fertility of the province of Gojjam.

The longer and more famous of these rivers, which he says is called Gehon in Scripture, was known to the Ethiopians as the Abbai. Paez is referring to the Book of Genesis, which has the verse, 'The name of the second river is Gehon: it is the one that flows round the whole of Ethiopia.' This river rises, he says, in the kingdom of Gojjam in that part called Sahala, whose inhabitants are called the Agau: they are Christians, though in the course of time they have been affected by superstitions and corrupted by gentiles and by their pagan neighbours, from whom they differ but little. The source of the Nile is situated in the eastern part of this kingdom at the head of a valley resembling a vast field surrounded on all sides by high mountain peaks.'

Paez was here on 21 April 1618 with Susenyos and his army. As he approached the source to examine it he saw two springs, circular in shape, both some four palms in diameter. 'I confess my joy,' he says, 'in seeing what in ancient times Cyprus and his son Cambyses and Alexander the Great and the famous Julius Caesar so much desired to know.' He knew his history well. Cambyses* had expended time, men and money to discover the source of the Nile, only to have his expedition defeated by the desert after many

---

* Cambyses II (died 521 B.C.), the son and successor of Cyrus the Great, King of ancient Persia, invaded Egypt in 525 B.C. After sacking Memphis he planned further conquests in Africa but was frustrated by a revolt at home.

hazards. Alexander the Great had sought the solution from the oracle of Jupiter Ammon but, complying with its direction, found the source of the Indus. Ptolemy Philadelphus,* hoping to trace the river to its source, had contemplated war on the Negus of Ethiopia. The Roman historian Lucian writes that Caesar would have preferred the renown of finding the source to his victories in civil wars. When they all failed, it was believed that the Nile rose in some impenetrable recesses of Africa.

The spring that is the source of the Blue Nile is at Ghish, seventy miles south of Lake Tana, on the summit of a hillock that stands in the centre of a great swamp, over 9,000 feet above sea level. To the west of the spring and eight hundred feet above it is Ghish mountain, which gives a view to the north of a range of hills running south to north and fading in the far distance, marking the edge of the escarpment of the high Ethiopian plateau. No flow of water can be seen at the spring, but it seeps through the swampy ground to a point down the slope where it forms a small brook.

On 4 November 1770, more than a century and half later, James Bruce of Kinnaird, the first Briton to travel in Ethiopia after the Jesuits had left, stood on this spot. He had come with the declared purpose of discovering the source of the Nile and was therefore compelled to claim what Paez had never claimed, that he was the first European to have found the springs of the great river.

Paez merely stated that he had been there and had tried to record what he saw as accurately as possible in his day. By contrast Bruce boasted he had discovered 'that spot which had baffled the genius, industry and inquiry of both ancients and moderns for the course of nearly three thousand years'. He goes on: 'though a mere private Briton, I triumphed here in my own mind over kings and their armies'. In his ecstasy he picked up half a coconut shell, drank from it some water from the spring, which Paez also had found so refreshing, and then toasted George III and a long line of princes. Two medallions were engraved to commemorate Bruce's discovery: the face of one has the image of Bruce; the other shows a radiant nymph in the act of uncovering to the explorer the veiled head of the ancient Nile lying at full length over three amphorae, from which water is pouring. Above is the inscription from the last great poet of the

* Ptolemy Philadelphus (c. 308-246 B.C.), King of ancient Egypt, was interested in the Nile, which he linked by a canal with the Red Sea.

heathen world, Claudian: '*Nec contingit ulli hoc vidisse caput*' ('None had the fortune to see this spring'), and the date, A.D. 1770.

Paez had been in this area without leisure to examine the source of the river as early as 1605, when on his pastoral visit to the Portuguese he had narrowly escaped an ambush laid by the Agau. In a letter written at this time to his friend Iturén he makes mention of the source as something well known, when he describes the movements of Ras Selasse's rebel forces against the Emperor Za Dengel. Since he may well have been there at other times also without examining the springs, it is understandable that he never made any claim to have discovered them.

In his refutation of Paez's supposed claim to the discovery, Bruce places the event in Za Dengel's reign and is right to the extent that Paez first heard about the source of the Blue Nile then. He asserts:

> No Portuguese, not Covillan, nor Rodrigo de Lima,* not Christovão da Gama, nor even the Patriarch Mendes saw the source of the Nile, nor has any one of them claimed to have seen it. The honour of having made the discovery is attributed to Paez. I came to examine into these pretentions to see if they were well founded. . . . They are without foundation since Paez in the *History* he wrote of Abssinia has not one word about the discovery.'

This, of course, is untrue. Moreover, when Bruce wrote there had already been published by order of the Royal Society as early as 1669 a number of essays by the Jesuit Jeronimo Lobo, who after Paez's death worked for a short time in this part of Ethiopia and had described the springs. Bruce would also have had before him the new and detailed edition of D'Anville's map of Africa, which was based on an accurate study of Paez's writings and marked fairly exactly the source of the Blue Nile. It need hardly be added that Bruce had not discovered, nor had Paez described, the source of the Nile. Both were on the wrong river. The true source is Lake Victoria a thousand miles away.

Several Portuguese had also visited the springs of the Blue Nile before Paez had done. After the death of da Gama many of them had first been settled on the frontiers of Adal and of Doaro, the Muslim state in which Harar was situated; they were later transferred by Sarsa Dengel to the borders of the Agau at Nanina in Damot, only

---

* Pero da Covilhã reached Ethiopia about 1490 and was still there when Dom Rodrigo da Lima, leader of the Portuguese embassy, arrived in 1520.

thirty miles from the source of the Abbai. Paez must have learnt all this from his friend João Gabriel, the leader of the Portuguese community, a man acquainted with all the provinces of the empire and highly esteemed by Jesuit writers for his integrity and intelligence. He also told Paez about the curious fish that could be unearthed alive from the dried-up bed of the river Mareb in Tigre: in spring it was a stream carrying little water, but near Debaroa it received a tributary that made it a considerable river after the rains. Gabriel also described to him how in company with others he had seen above the source of the Abbai the fiery exhalations that came from the pagan sacrifices there. His description was published in Portugal as early as 1614.

Paez's account of the springs was published in 1678 by Athanasius Kircher, the professor of science and mathematics at the Jesuit Roman College, in his celebrated *Mundus Subterraneus*.* Kircher had before him the text of Paez's *History* in manuscript and had translated it from Portuguese into Latin. Through the wide circulation of Kircher's work it came about that Paez received credit for the discovery. Kircher gives high praise to Paez, not as explorer, but simply for his painstaking description. 'He noted down,' says Kircher, 'with such great diligence every detail . . . that henceforth we should stand by his testimony, confirmed by the Emperor, that the source of the Nile has now been established with infallible certainty.'

Paez's description, on which Kircher stakes his credit, continues:

> The water from the spring is very clear and soft and most pleasant in savour. It is noteworthy that the two eyes of the spring do not come out on the plain at the top of the mountain, but as its foot. I also probed the depth of the fountains; at the first I put down a lance which, entering some eleven palms, seemed to touch some sort of roots of nearby trees very intricately enmeshed with one another.
>
> The second spring is a stone throw's distance from the first. In trying to establish its depth I inserted a lance twelve palms in length and found no bottom; then with two lances fastened together, twenty palms in all, I tried again, but even then I could not reach the bottom. The inhabitants say that the whole mountain is full of water and as proof of this they point out that the entire plain is moist and boils under foot, an evident sign of hidden waters, and for this reason the

---

* *Mundus Subterraneus in XII Libros digestus*, 2 vols., Amsterdam, 1665.

water does not pour out of the spring, but goes down with great force to the roots, as the natives affirmed . . . The Emperor said that the earth moved very little that year [1618] because of the great drought but that in other years it shook and steamed to such an extent that it could only be approached with peril. The perimeter of the place forms a kind of circular lake, its latitude about the distance a javelin can be hurled.

Below the summit of this mountain, about a league distant to the east, live a people called Guix . . . .. There is in this place a village of gentiles who sacrifice a large number of cows and come to the springs at a certain time every year with a man they regard as their high priest, who sacrifices one cow near the spring, then throws its head to the bottom.

Entering into greater detail, Lobo says that Guix is the name of the village through which the path to the summit lies, adding that everyone sacrificed one or more cows according to the degree of his wealth or devotion. In his time the bones of these cows already formed two 'mountains of considerable height', which he took as proof that these people had paid homage to the river for a long time. During the ritual the priest annointed himself with the grease and tallow of the cows and harangued the bystanders, 'confirming them in their ignorance and superstition'.

Today, on the ridge of Ghish mountain overlooking the springs, is a church dedicated to St Michael and the Ethiopian Saint Zarabruk, where the priests who serve it have the exclusive right to draw the waters of the source. It is generally believed that the church was built in the reign of John I, who died exactly sixty years after Paez, but it is said by others to have been founded by Susenyos when he was here with Paez, perhaps with the purpose of making it a place of Christian rather than heathen worship.

Bruce, passing through Italy on his return from Ethiopia in 1774, claimed that he had consulted Paez's book in three copies – in Rome, Bologna and Milan. He said he had found in none any mention of the discovery of the source of the Nile; but in fact the book was extant only in the single manuscript that Kircher had used, which at the time of the suppression of the Jesuits in 1773 had become the property of the Papal government. All Bruce could have had before him was Kircher's translation, about which he wrote:

I shall now state, in Kircher's own words, translated into English, the description he has given as from Paez, and I will fairly submit to any

109

reader of judgment whether this is a description he ought to be content with from an eyewitness; whether it may not suit the sources of any other river as well as those of the Nile; or whether in itself it is distinct enough to leave a clear idea behind it.

Bruce's translation is significantly incomplete. In order to bolster his thesis that Paez must have discovered the source of some small stream, he omits from Kircher the passage describing how the Jesuit probed the depth of the springs, and also the mention of the sacrifices near them which indicated that from time immemorial the site had been regarded as sacred. It has even been suggested that he had not seen Kircher but only *A New History of Ethiopia*, the translation of a work by a German, H. Ludolf, published in 1681 at Frankfurt. Both made the same error of transcribing Sahala, a district in Gojjam, as Sabala.

In contrast with Bruce, Paez was more interested in plotting the course of the Blue Nile than in its source. In this he was unquestionably a pioneer. His presence with the Emperor in the field during several campaigns gave him an opportunity to do this, for he was frequently crossing territory that had only recently been cleared of hostile forces. He tells how the Little Abbai, on leaving the springs, is joined by the Jamma, the Branty, the Kelti and other streams until three days' march from its source it becomes such a broad river 'that a ball shot from a musket will hardly get across from one side to the other'.

He states accurately that the Blue Nile, passing some forty miles through Tana, leaves the lake as the Great Abbai, reaching the Tisisat Falls some fifteen miles further on. He makes it clear that it is the only river that flows out of Tana, thus correcting the well-known Flemish geographer Gerhard Kremer, better known as Gerardus Mercator, who devised the map on which meridians of longitude are drawn at right angles to the parallels of latitude. Kremer believed that the Zaïre rose in the lake and thus gave rise to the hope that Ethiopia might be reached from the Congo.

Perhaps ten years after Paez, Jeronimo Lobo also followed the Great Abbai until he reached the Tisisat Falls, which he says are among the most beautiful in the world. He describes how the beams of the sun paint a thousand rainbows on the water and the mist rising from this fall 'may be seen farther than the noise can be heard'. He continues:

After this cataract the Nile again collects its scattered stream among

110

the rocks, which seem to be disjoined in this place only to afford it a passage. They are so near each other that in my time a bridge was laid over them. Sultan Segued [Susenyos] has built a bridge here . . . which is the first the Abyssinians have seen on the Nile and very much facilitates communication between the provinces and encourages commerce among the inhabitants of this empire.

James Bruce, referring to the Falls, speaks of them as one of 'the most magnificent, stupendous sights in creation much degraded and vilified by the lies of a grovelling priest'. This reference to Lobo is all the more difficult to understand because in fact the Jesuit came closer to measuring the Falls correctly than did Bruce, who put them at less than one third of their true height.* Lobo stated that he clambered on to a ledge of rock below the Falls from which he looked up at the cascading water and saw rainbows in the gorge. This description was dismissed by Bruce as a 'downright falsehood' on the ground that no one could have reached the ledge through the thundering water:

> And supposing the friar placed in his imaginary seat under the curve of the immense arch of water, he must have had a portion of firmness more than falls to the share of an ordinary man, and which is not likely to be acquired in a monastic life, to philosophize upon optics in such a situation, where everything would seem to his dazzled eyes to be in motion, and the stream, in a noise like the loudest thunder, to make the solid rock (at least as to sense) shake to its very foundation, and threaten to tear every nerve to pieces, and to deprive one of the other senses beside that of hearing.

But Bruce arrived at the Tisisat Falls when the river was in flood; Lobo was there at Christmas, the height of the dry season. When Cheesman visited the Falls in May 1926, he sat exactly where Lobo had sat three hundred years earlier.

From Tisisat, Paez goes on to trace the Great Abbai through Begameder, Amhara and Damot back into Gojjam to within a short day's journey of its source. He reckoned that it took twenty-nine days to follow its course round Gojjam alone.

Neither Paez nor Lobo pretended to any knowledge of the river

* The Falls which Bruce calls 'the most magnificent sight I have ever seen', are second only in Africa to the Zambesi Falls. Lobo put their height at fifty feet, Bruce at only forty. The true drop is 150 feet. Alan Moorhead, *The Blue Nile (London 1962)*, 24.

beyond the frontiers of Ethiopia. In 1615, three years before Paez visited the source, Cela Krestos, at the head of his army, had crossed into Ombarea and Faxcalo* where, 'being able to get no intelligence on the condition of the people and astonished at their unbounded extent, he returned without daring to attempt anything'. They did not know that the river flowed another thousand miles before joining the White Nile at Khartoum.

To this time belongs Paez's encounter with the 'torpedo' fish which, he says, people call the *adenguez* or the 'terror', a name given it because it causes the fisherman who catches it to tremble in all his bones. He tells how João Gabriel, sitting once on a river bank with some friends, hooked a fish one palm in length which had no scales, looked like a dog fish and came out of the water without wriggling. When Gabriel took it into his hands to extract the hook, he instantly dropped the fish and began trembling all over: his teeth started to rattle, he became unconscious and would have fallen into the river had he not been seated at the time. On recovering his senses he realized what had happened, summoned a servant and ordered him to extract the hook from the fish. When the man took the fish in his hands he too started to tremble and fell unconscious.

When he rose he asked Gabriel, 'What did I do, sir, that you struck me down?'

The captain laughed, as did the others present, when they realized that he did not know how it happened. All then waited until the fish was dead before taking out the hook. Paez says that there were other Portuguese who caught fish of this kind, one of which was a *covado* in length.

In addition, Jeronimo Lobo observed that close to where the Nile leaves Ethiopia, 'a region where neither Greeks nor Romans had penetrated', there were few fish to be found in the river. He explains this by the number of cataracts 'down which the fish cannot fall without being killed' and by presence of the crocodile, which he found 'very ugly, having no proportion between its length and thickness'. Although, as he points out, others had described the crocodile, Lobo asked to be excused for writing about the animal

* Faxcalo is on the Blue Nile about a hundred and eighty miles south of Sennar; Ombarea, the name given by the Jesuits to the district south of Askuna, lies between the Sori and Dura rivers. Paez calls it the 'kingdom opposite the kingdom of Fazogli'.

again on the plea that the Nile contained at least as many as any other river in the world. The crocodile, he says,

> hath short feet, a wide mouth, with two rows of sharp teeth, standing wide from each other, a brown skin fortified with scales even to his nose that a musket ball cannot penetrate it. His sight is extremely quick and at a great distance. In the water he is daring and fierce and will seize on any that are so unfortunate as to be found by him bathing, who, if they escape with life, are almost sure to leave some limb in his mouth. Neither I, nor any with whom I have conversed about the crocodile, have ever seen him weep, and therefore I take this liberty of ranking all that has been told us of his tears among the fables that are proper only to amuse children.

This passage gave particular pleasure to Samuel Johnson when he was engaged in translating Lobo's book of travels. He praised the Jesuit for qualities he was later to find lacking in James Bruce:

> He [Lobo] appears by his modest and disaffected narration to have described things as he saw them, to have copied nature from life and to have consulted his senses, not his imagination. He meets with no basilisks that destroy the eyes, his crocodiles devour their prey without tears, his cataracts fall from the rock without deafening the inhabitants.

It is unfortunate that Paez's book was not available to Johnson, for Paez wrote even more scientifically than Lobo did. Paez himself concludes his few pages on the Nile with an account of all the fish to be found in the river.

Lobo, perhaps more excited than Paez at seeing the springs of the Blue Nile, regrets that persons exist who are 'so bigoted as not to have any regard to people who have been on the spot and by the evidence of their eyes can confute all that the ancients have written'. He asserted that it was difficult, probably impossible, to reach the source by tracing the river from its mouth, for all who have attempted it had been stopped by the cataracts. 'Imagining that none who followed them could pass any further, they have taken the liberty of entertaining us with their own fictions.'

James Bruce tried to do precisely this in his first attempt to reach the source of the Blue Nile, but found his progress blocked at Aswan by tribal wars. He then set out from Massawa. He might have saved himself the trouble and expense had he taken the advice of Lobo, whom he was determined to denigrate. Lobo had written of earlier expeditions to reach the source:

> If these men who endeavoured to discover the spring of this river had landed at Massawa and had marched a little more to the south than the south-west, they might perhaps have gratified their curiosity at less expense and in about twenty days might have enjoyed the desired sight of the sources of the Nile.

In his expedition Bruce added very greatly to the knowledge of Ethiopia then available in England and had no need to assert that the distances, heights and place names given by either Paez or Lobo were incorrect in order to establish his claim to have discovered the source of the river Nile.

7

During Fernandes's absence on his abortive attempt to reach Melinde, the Emperor's brother, Cela Krestos, fell sick on a visit to court. While engaged in one of the theological debates there he felt a fever gripping him. He sought out Paez, who told him that in Spain the customary remedy was to bleed the patient five or six times in the course of a week. The Emperor approved the treatment, and he gave orders for his brother to be given sugared barley, which Paez also prescribed, instead of mulled wine which was the standard Ethiopian remedy. It was a bold decision, since the Ethiopians resisted change in the application of medicines as much as they did in matters of religion. Nevertheless Susenyos was anxious: he knew that if his brother died, this would be interpreted as a divine punishment for his support of the Jesuits.

All through the Prince's illness Paez remained at his bedside. 'I was never separated from him,' he wrote. On the fifth day, after four bleedings, and at the height of his fever, Cela Krestos turned to Paez:

'I see that I am dying,' he said, 'but I am not at all afraid, for in my soul I know that I have remained true to our faith.'

Cela Krestos feared only for Paez's life. He was worried that the monks would bring about the Jesuit's death through the power of their prayers, which were then being recited in their monasteries. It was a popular belief, derived from the Old Testament, that if God were asked to avenge himself on his enemies, then they would certainly die. Cela Krestos had heard that the monks were already calling on God for the death of Paez and were preparing for war, removing the altars, replicas of the ark, from their churches and carrying them on their heads for their own protection, as they always did in battle.

115

When news of this reached the Emperor's mother, she wrote to Cela Krestos imploring him to return to the Alexandrine faith to save himself from a worse fate. But her son only scoffed at the credulity of people who were ready to believe anything the monks chose to tell them. He was anxious, however, to make a full confession of his life. 'I told him,' writes Paez,

> that while it was a good thing to confess, he did not appear to be as close to his end as he thought. Every hour the Emperor was enquiring after his brother . . . and he came at night to visit him. When Cela Krestos was feeling better he said he would postpone his confession until he could make it with more preparation and concentration. On the eighth day the last traces of the fever left him. When the Emperor came again, his joy was boundless. The three of us were alone that evening and spoke about matters of faith until after midnight when the Emperor left and I returned to my tent.

This may well have been the deciding moment in Susenyos's approach to the Roman Church. 'The Emperor,' says Paez, 'was very pleased with the way I had remained at his brother's side. He told me that he would have died if I had not been there, and that he could never repay me for the love I had shown him.' Paez added that he had never ceased praying for Cela Krestos during his illness.

News of Fernandes's embassy had not been kept secret from the Abuna Simon. At the instigation of the monks at court Simon pronounced excommunications once more against all, the Emperor not excepted, who should hold that there was more than one nature in Christ. Paez responded by asking Simon to explain why he now declared the contrary to what he had only recently openly professed after prolonged consultations. He demanded to know whether anything had come to light in the interval to account for this reversal of opinion, for there were many now under an earlier excommunication for holding the opposite position, which had been reached after tedious discussions. The Abuna Simon answered cryptically that he had been made to drink 'sugared water administered with deadly poison in a golden cup'. When pressed, he refused to say more.

Meanwhile the Emperor's position had crystallized. In July 1614 he sent further letters to Paul V and Philip III, despatching them this time via Arquico and the caravan route to Cairo, where the French Consul forwarded them to Rome. Explaining that his ambassador and Fernandes had been frustrated by Moors in their attempt to reach Melinde, he presented this as a further reason for obtaining urgent military assistance. Paul V was impressed. On 11 December 1616 he wrote to the Catholic King endorsing Susenyos's request: 'It is hardly needful for Us to press this business since . . . it is a question of the salvation of almost innumerable souls, who are a pressing concern of Ours'; he added that he had written to his Nuncio in Spain asking him to pursue the business in detail with the King. Philip III was quick to act. On 21 February 1617 he instructed the Viceroy of India to report on the feasibility of establishing contact with Ethiopia via Melinde, the route that Fernandes had attempted in reverse. In his turn, the Viceroy ordered the captain of the fortress of Melinde, Simão de Mello Pereira, to survey all possible trails into the interior from the east coast. Then on 1 March 1617 the King promised military aid to Susenyos provided the situation in India allowed the despatch of troops.

Resolved to unite his Church with Rome, the Emperor had been prepared by Paez to face the obstructions that beset him on several sides. But he assured Paez that he now enjoyed deep peace within himself. At the same time he was anxious to keep Paez at court where he could supervise the food sent to his hut to make sure it was not poisoned. As a further safeguard he asked a widowed lady of the imperial family to leave her lodgings so that Paez could move in, but since a large number of her female attendants would have had to remain in residence, Paez declined the offer.

The favour shown by Susenyos to the Jesuits inevitably roused the jealousy of the monks, who now worked on the people to revolt. In an attempt to forestall trouble the Emperor summoned for September 1614 all the monastic superiors and scholars in Gojjam, Begameder and Dambia to meet him for what he hoped would be a definitive theological disputation. The reaction was predictable. Rather than attend, the supporters of the Patriarch proclaimed everywhere their readiness to die for their traditional faith, while the monks were reported again to be practising arms drill in readiness for battle.

The Emperor was unperturbed. At court he showed where his sympathies lay by proposing that Portuguese dress should replace the Turkish-style *cabayas*. He asked to have a number of ruffs tailored, got Cela Krestos to wear one, and on the feast of the nativity of Our Lady he and his courtiers came to Mass dressed in them. Paez was uneasy but the people were so impressed that they proposed that the ruffs should be worn only by the Emperor; others complained that Susenyos was aping the Portuguese in clothing as well as in religion.*

On Cela Krestos's arrival for the congress Paez visited him every day, for with him had come the principal monks of the province of Gojjam, whom he had won over to the Roman position. In their presence Bella Krestos, the Emperor's half-brother, brought out certain old books in which a number of phrases incompatible with the monophysite tenets had been deleted. When Susenyos was shown them, he asked Bella Krestos to research further into the main calumnies against the Roman faith and provide an answer.

On the day appointed for the meeting the Abuna Simon arrived with an immense company of monks and superiors of monasteries – so numerous, says Paez, that 'all you could see at the Emperor's court were squadrons of monks and, with them wandering wherever they pleased, a crowd of nuns, looking more like *beatae* than religious, all resolved to die for their old faith'. Their mood was so hostile that Paez was again told his life was in peril and was advised to flee. He refused, not because he courted martyrdom, but because he judged his presence was needed to encourage the Emperor's supporters. He wanted to demonstrate peacefully that Scripture, the Fathers, theological reasoning and the schools of Rome and Byzantium upheld his position.

The first encounter between the Emperor and the Abuna Simon was stormy. In front of the entire gathering Susenyos upbraided the Patriarch for abjuring his solemn affirmation that in Christ there were two natures. When Simon denied that he had done any such thing, Susenyos threatened to depose him. After sending for Cela Krestos, the Emperor went with him to meet the Abuna a second time. As the debate was renewed the crowd shouted in unison that the Abuna had been denied the right to make himself heard. Uproar followed, and Simon again declared his loathing for the Emperor and publicly excommunicated him. For the Abuna the question of one or two natures in Christ was a matter to be settled by arms, not

---

* In some Japanese paintings of this period certain nobles and their retinues are depicted in a modified form of European dress, with ruffs and baggy zouave-like mosquito-proof trousers, a rosary round their neck and a crucifix hanging from their waist. This fashion was not restricted to Christian converts. Cf. C. F. Boxer, 'Portuguese Influence in Japan in the 16th and 17th Centuries' in *Japan Society*, Vol. XXXIII, 51.

by reason: God would be with the victor. No credence could be given to the new translation of St Paul or to any of the Roman books.

The demonstration became a rebellion. Cela Krestos was for executing the ring-leaders on the spot, but the Emperor favoured compromise. However, he insisted that since the doctrine of the two natures of Christ was to be found in the Ethiopian books, it must be held by all: it was expressed in the word *Bahari*, which had always been accepted. As has been pointed out,* the doctrine of the two natures in Christ, which Susenyos put before the crowd, could not be satisfactorily explained without the use of Greek terminology, in which it was originally formulated at Chalcedon; Amharic was a far from adequate language for the discussion of such problems. Bruce rightly remarks of the words for 'nature' and 'person':

> Neither of them has ever been translated into Abyssinian so as to mean the same thing in different places . . . . The two natures in Christ, the two persons, their unity . . . are all wrapped up in ten-fold darkness and [are] inextricable from amidst the thick clouds of heresy and ignorance of language. Nature is often mistaken for person and person for nature; the same of the human substance. It is monstrous to hear their reasoning upon it. One would think that every different monk, every time he talks, purposely broaches some new heresy.

For a while after the Emperor had resorted to the word *Bahari*, the rebels were appeased. Then a report spread that they had been outmanoeuvred, and the rising began in earnest.

Already the Abuna Simon had approached a Jew to succeed Susenyos as Emperor. 'These Jews,' Paez writes, 'live on high and precipitous mountains in natural fastnesses that are impossible of access.' Called also Falashas, they belonged to an indigenous race of pre-Christian times and spoke an Hamitic tongue. They had formerly possessed large tracts of land including almost the whole district of Dambea and the province of Wagara to the north-east of Lake Tana. Some of them at this time had been converted to Christianity. When the Galla invasions contracted the frontiers of the empire, they had gradually been driven out. But they had then defended themselves courageously in the Semen mountain range, where they earned a living by making darts, ploughs and other instruments;

* Beckingham and Huntingford, *Some Records*, xxiv.

119

crafts which were regarded as degrading by the Ethiopians, who themselves lived either by farming or soldiering.

After a brief diversion to hold back a fresh Galla attack Susenyos marched against the pretender – 'the chieftain holding dominion over all the Jews'. No fighting was necessary for one of their number named Gedeon betrayed him to the Emperor, who cut off his head and set it up for all to see. Bella Krestos had joined the march, but on returning to his province became sick, called to pay his respects to the Fathers at Gorgora and remained with them a month. His death shortly afterwards was a setback for the Jesuits. From the beginning he had been strongly attached to the Roman cause and at the same time was greatly respected by the monks; he had helped in discussions by distinguishing between certain 'grave errors' of the Ethiopian Church and others 'less grave'. The first of the royal circle to proclaim himself a Roman Catholic, he had defended the doctrine, moral teaching and ecclesiastical customs of his adopted Church in the presence of the Emperor. He had also complied with his wish to write a treatise against the Ethiopian errors and had advised him on his approach to the Holy See.

Although for a while the rebellion instigated by the Abuna Simon was suppressed, the Alexandrine party continued to incite the people against the Jesuits. They were supported in Tigre by the Viceroy, the Emperor's son-in-law, 'a man with no knowledge of books', as Paez describes him, 'who was easily suborned'. At his instigation the governor of the province ordered all the Portuguese to be stripped of their lands; those married to Ethiopian women were to forfeit half their estates and surrender the other half to their wives: should these wives revert to the Roman faith they were to lose their nose and ears. The execution of these decrees was entrusted to two officials who acted with extreme barbarity.

Without success Fr. Lorenzo Romano at Fremona tried through his friends in Tigre to soften the impact of the persecution. Paez, who was at court, on receiving his report sought out the Emperor as he was about to attend Mass with his courtiers. 'He seated himself,' wrote Paez, 'and gave me an audience. He heard me with much show of feeling and was unable to restrain his tears.' Cela Krestos suspected a plot in Tigre to remove the Emperor. He proved in fact to be right. Susenyos tracked down the men who had incited the Viceroy to rebellion. In conversation with Paez he spoke about his predecessor, Za Dengel, who had been forced from the throne and killed because he had abandoned precipitately the ancient faith of Ethiopia. He said, 'They would like to see the same thing happen to me. If God so wishes it, let his holy will be done. If not, there is no harm they can do me.'

Paez kissed Susenyos's hand, remarking that it was only his strong action that was holding the Empire together: it might at any time splinter into autonomous regions over which local rulers were already claiming independent jurisdiction. The Emperor then dictated a reprimand to the Viceroy of Tigre, who replied that Susenyos had been misinformed. Rejecting the explanation, Susenyos gave orders for all confiscated property to be returned and for the Governor's officials to be punished. Paez in his letter reporting these events to the Jesuit General marvelled at the terror the Emperor was able to inspire in his subject princes. He also hinted that Susenyos had already determined to bring his people into union with Rome.

Paez continued to work with caution, seeking always to interpret correctly Ignatius's directives for the mission. At the conclusion of his letter from Gorgora in June 1616 he writes that he has just heard of the death of Acquaviva;* Paez asks the new General, Mutio Vitelleschi, to have special concern for Ethiopia, which had been a 'mission so near to Ignatius's heart' and to help 'further the requests of this good Emperor, Seltan Sagad, to his Holiness and to His Majesty [the King of Portugal], which will redound greatly to the benefit of the Catholic Church'. Speaking about himself, Paez complains that since the Emperor insists on having him at court, he can seldom get away to Fremona, a difficult and dangerous journey of fifteen days, though he could visit Collela more frequently, which was no more than six days on an easy road. Probably for this reason in the next year he was succeeded as Superior by Fernandes, who would have had less difficulty in attending to the requirements of the few scattered Jesuits in the country.

In none of his letters did Paez ask for more Jesuits to be sent to the mission, for such a step would only excite the fears of the Alexandrine monks. At no time during his years in Ethiopia were there more than six priests in the country, usually two at each of the three mission stations. The Fathers at Gorgora, where Paez and Fer-

* Claudio Acquaviva died on 31 January 1615. Mutio Vitelleschi, who was elected to succeed him on 15 November the same year, had been Rector of the English College, Rome.

nandes were based, attended the court; at Fremona, their work was principally among the Portuguese; at Collela they were engaged in the work of translation with the assistance provided by Cela Krestos. In all three centres they continued their discussions with the monks. In Fremona and Gorgora there were schools, called seminaries in the annual reports, primarily for the Portuguese and half-castes, but also for the occasional Ethiopian student. At Collela also the Fathers undertook the private education of a few Ethiopians; three of them, who were servants of Cela Krestos, were first taught to read and write Portuguese, then later, Latin.

After the Portuguese in Tigre had recovered their estates, the Fathers at Fremona were again harassed, this time by the Galla. In 1617 their partially fortified settlement was invested by some roving bands who tried to force the Fathers to surrender with all who had taken refuge with them. Afraid to assault the place directly, the Galla attempted to reduce it by diverting the stream that supplied its water. Striking a section of bronze piping which they took to be part of an engine of war, they fled, though not before they had set fire to some seventy houses in the district. That year the Emperor gave the Fathers two villages close to the Red Sea where they could receive safely the alms and stipends sent from India, and a third in the hills to serve as a refuge in time of danger. In fact there were few years in which they were safe from the Galla or the Turks. As one Father wrote, 'It is as if an axe were held above our neck and brought a little closer every year.'

With this further donation the Fathers now possessed nine villages or manors, but it made little difference to their finances owing to the system of land-holding. Not only did each manor carry with it the obligation of entertaining strangers, who were numerous in Tigre, but the method of accounting frequently made the manor unprofitable. The tenant farmer, when his harvest was ripe, called in the *chumo* or headman, entertained him lavishly, gave him a present, then showed him round the farm. If satisfied with his reception, this steward would make a declaration that the land which, for example, may have yielded five or six sacks of corn, had provided only that number of baskets or less. Since the Fathers had no choice but to work through the stewards, the manors did not bring them any real wealth. There were even years when they had to buy corn from other manors with alms sent from Goa.

The schools at Fremona and Gorgora catered only for small numbers. At Fremona there is mention also of a 'sodality' or pious association among the students, who went to neighbouring villages to teach children their catechism and acted also as companions to the Fathers on their pastoral excursions. The number of converts listed each year indicates again that their ministry was not directed to the native Ethiopians. For instance in 1614 at Gorgora, in spite of its proximity to the court, there were only fourteen converts. The breakdown for the year 1617 is interesting: of the forty-three received into the Roman Church only twenty-three were Ethiopians, the others included dark-skinned Jews and the son of a Portuguese who had gone over to the Alexandrine faith. Careful note, however, was taken of the contacts each house had with the monks of the district. There was an occasion when a distinguished monk came to Gorgora to discuss the usual question of the two natures in Christ, became ill and was cured by the medicines prescribed by the Fathers.

While no direct evangelization of the people was undertaken, much of the Fathers' time was taken up with visits to the Portuguese settled in outlying places on the frontiers. Reporting to Rome on their return, they expressed a number of times their distress at the way Ethiopians, adhering to the customs abandoned in the early Christian era, took their male children to be circumcised forty days, and girls eighty days, after birth, only then having them baptized. The result was that 'many died in original sin before the ceremony could be carried out'.

Following always the directives laid down by St Ignatius, Paez concentrated on the court, the nobles and persons of influence. It was the policy that Matteo Ricci had pursued with striking success in Peking. Already Paez had won the admiration of the Emperor, who had long since admitted the superiority of Roman teaching. On his side Paez found much to praise in Susenyos, writing: 'He is virtuous, and combines firmness with prudence, justice with mercy; he loves peace, punishes dissidents and trouble-makers, is sparing of wine (something uncommon among Ethiopians) and is also very intelligent.' Since he had been brought up in a remote area of the country, the Emperor lacked the more formal education of his brother Cela Krestos, who was better equipped when it came to theological debate.

Paez also drew encouragement from the comparatively recent success of a fellow Jesuit, Gian Battista Eliano, who in 1580 had brought back the Maronite Christians to their former union with Rome: like the Ethiopians they had been cut off for centuries from the West by Arab and later Turkish invasions. An ecumenical synod at the monastery of Qanobin in Syria had adjusted differences in the presentation of Christian doctrine and permitted the retention of many usages that had no unorthodox connotations. It was Paez's hope that a similar compromise might effect the same results in Ethiopia.

Circumcision, observance of the Sabbath and other Jewish customs were regarded by Ethiopians as proof that their faith derived from the eunuch, the treasurer of Queen Candace of Ethiopia, whom the deacon Philip overtook on the road from Jerusalem and baptized after interpreting the passage of Isaiah he was reading. 'It would be regarded as no less folly,' wrote one of the Jesuits, 'to deny that their Emperor descended from Solomon that it would be in Rome to say that the city was not built by Romulus and Remus, or in Spain that their kings did not descend from the Goths, or theirs in Portugal from King Alfonso Henriques.' Traditions of this kind formed such a substantial part of their religious heritage that any abrogation of an ancient custom was sufficient to kindle a rebellion. Paez understood this and ceaselessly urged the Emperor to respect rites that did not conflict with established Roman teaching. He and other Jesuits admitted that in their study of Ethiopian practices taken from the Judaic law they had for the first time understood several passages in the Bible.

Contact with the imperial family was maintained in all the Jesuit centres. In 1613, while Fernandes was searching for a route to Melinde, Julius, a son-in-law of the Emperor, visited Fremona, dined with the Jesuit community, was shown their chapel dedicated to the Holy Cross, and expressed his delight with the devotional statues that adorned it. On this occasion he renewed the privileges of the Fathers that his predecessor had revoked. At Collela, Cela Krestos, whenever he had leisure, visited the Fathers and confessed and received communion there in the presence of a large number of his followers. Out of his private resources he paid four monks and four *dabtara* to assist in translations and himself composed a number of songs in praise of the two natures of Christ which boys sang in the villages of his province. Following the Roman custom, he fasted every Wednesday and Friday and exhorted his courtiers to do the same. He once asked a Father to settle a scruple of conscience he had concerning the purchase and sale of slaves. The issue was then raised with the Emperor who, after consulting Paez, summoned the province governors and ordered them under penalty of death and confiscation of their property to forbid his subjects to have any traffic whatever in slaves with either Moors or Turks. But after Susenyos's death the trade was revived and flourished well into the twentieth century.

In the imperial camp, which in fact was the court on the march, the Fathers served as chaplains to Cela Krestos. They would seem also to have ministered to the troops, to the fury of the monks, who during a campaign in 1619 against the Galla threatened to incite the army to rebellion. Paez again counselled caution, and on this occasion as at other times proposed that in all religious matters the people should be given liberty of conscience. He supported the Emperor when he issued a decree withdrawing permission to the Fathers to serve the troops spiritually. However when Cela Krestos reprimanded his brother for this in two letters, he replied that he had to bow to the storm but hinted at the same time that his orders need not be rigidly enforced.

With the help given him by Cela Krestos, Fernandes on his return to Gojjam resumed work on the translation of several devotional and theological books. He also revised the Ethiopic missal and manuals of doctrine, compiled a handbook of cases of conscience for the Ethiopian clergy, and wrote a life of the Blessed Virgin.* To enable Fernandes to purchase parchment Cela Krestos detached some clasps from the golden chain around his neck and gave them to him. This was the time when nobles, dressing in Turkish style, wore necklaces and bracelets of gold and had waist girdles or sashes containing large golden pieces.

In 1617 Paez sought permission from the Emperor to build a new church in the European style. The suggestion came from Cela Krestos who admired the chapel the Fathers had built at Gorgora: he was ready to defray the expenses of the building and ornamentation and

---

* During his years of exile in India after the expulsion of the Jesuits Fernandes saw to the publication of his treatise on the errors of the Ethiopian Church. In his Amharic he was assisted by some Ethiopians who had accompanied him to Goa. The Pope sent Ethiopic types from Italy and the work was printed at St Paul's College. There is a copy of this book in the Biblioteca Naçional in Lisbon.

also to provide damask for its furnishings, asking in return only a statue of Our Lady of the Assumption from the General of the Jesuits. Cela Krestos showed Paez where he could quarry fine stone, both white and reddish, on land already given to the Jesuits; they were unaware it was to be found there since it was covered by a deep layer of top soil.

The site of the church remained to be chosen. Paez's first plan was to acquire a property adjoining the Jesuit estate, but the Emperor intervened. He came himself to see the Fathers. Entering their chapel he took off his shoes, asked to hear Mass and a sermon and was persuaded by Paez to remain and eat with them.

'The day is advanced,' Paez remarked, 'the sun is high, you should not go out without eating.' Warned of his coming, Paez had dressed two chickens.

The Emperor ate very little but all that remained was given to his courtiers. He then went with Paez to find a satisfactory site. 'Here,' he said, pointing to a lie of land that pleased him, 'here you will build your church. You may take all this land,' he added with a gesture. 'And I shall give other and better land to the prince who owns it.' This Susenyos did, then returned to his tent which was set up in a remote field, for fever was raging at court.

'Our friends were delighted,' Paez wrote to the Jesuit General, 'but our enemies were angered that the Emperor had demeaned himself to the extent of actually eating with us and personally seeking out a site.' Paez was overjoyed. The position was healthy and the soil produced everything in abundance, whereas the first location he had chosen was unhealthy.

Paez proposed to start building immediately and set about cutting the stone. But Susenyos needed his assistance for a much grander project: he had decided to build a permanent capital of the empire. Accompanying the Emperor to a number of proposed sites, Paez rejected them all. Finally he settled on one of his own choice, which was cool in summer and mild in winter. The area was marked out on the system followed by the Emperor when he pitched his camp on the march. Paez was allotted some ground close to the Emperor's compound, and a large area was assigned to the Portuguese who were left to divide it among themselves.

Paez's account lacks topographical precision, but the site is almost certainly that of Gondar, the first fixed capital of the empire, which was built by Susenyos's son, Fasiladas. Paez says that when he was surveying the whole area he viewed the countryside from an eminence that might well have been the site on which the palace was built in the next reign. Certainly the lay-out of Gondar corresponds with the scant information of Susenyos's proposed city given by Paez, who had experience of planning both at Fremona and Collela. Here Paez would seem to have followed the principles of choice that governed his work there. Gondar was surrounded by high mountains, affording it military protection; it enjoyed an intermediate altitude and so escaped extremes of temperature; and there was water in plenty from two streams encircling the site. The rains were adequate and the soil produced two or sometimes three crops a year. As in the camp, Gondar was divided into several quarters each of which pursued its own life. The imperial compound was eventually walled off; the nobility had their own quarters with well-spaced houses each with its garden, and the clergy theirs in which the Abuna and the *echage* were given detached enclosures. It was to become one of the few centres of population that grew beyond the size of a village.

Another illustration of the Emperor's dependence on Paez occurred the following year. Late in 1618 Susenyos called on him to interpret the significance of a comet that first appeared above Tana on 9 November. 'It was seen in the west,' wrote Paez,

> and the light it shed formed a column like a very clear vapour, not in a straight line, but inclined to the south. The tail made a complete turn towards the north forming a kind of arc. It could be seen for two hours before dawn and then disappeared suddenly from view as soon as the sun started to rise. One day the Emperor summoned me as it appeared and we watched it together from the patio of his palace until it could be seen no longer. Later he summoned the nobles of his own court and in front of them all asked me whether or not it portended some punishment of God.

In reply Paez instanced examples from Scriptures: God, he said, gave a sign to the Jews before Antiochus sacked Jerusalem — for forty consecutive days troops of armed men appeared in the sky. And according to St Gregory, signs were seen in the heavens before the barbarians entered Italy. In his own day he himself had observed a comet which pointed for several days towards Portugal at the time Dom Sebastian crossed to Africa, where many nobles of the kingdom fell in battle.* When God was angry with his people he gave these signs so that they might repent, do penance and avert his punishments. In conclusion Paez cited the psalm '*Dedisti metuentibus te significationem ut fugiant a facie arcus*' ('You have given to those who fear you a sign that they may fly from the bow that threatens them').†

Even after the Emperor had donated the site for the new church he urged Paez to make certain he could not find a better one elsewhere. If he did, Susenyos undertook to let him have it with the surrounding land; he knew that Paez's numerous excursions to the Portuguese had made him well acquainted with the countryside. Susenyos laid down one condition, however: in the construction of the church only cedar wood was to be used. This involved a difficulty, since cedars grew only on the properties belonging to monks. Although the Emperor paid them compensation when he ordered it to be cut down, the owners grumbled. Far from taking notice of this, Susenyos ordered the best trees to be felled. Altogether forty-eight *cobades* of fine, straight cedar were presented to Paez.

The foundation stone was laid with great solemnity two days before Christmas 1617. Work was slow. The following June, Paez wrote: 'Until now it is not more than fourteen hands high. Winter has begun and I have had to go to court frequently at the request of the Emperor and some grandees. They call on me whenever there is a matter which they cannot settle among themselves.' On 9 November 1620 the cornerstone was laid by the Emperor himself

---

* Sebastian, King of Portugal (1557-78), grandson and successor of John III. He set out in 1578 with a large force of foreign mercenaries for Morocco, where at the Battle of the Three Kings at Alcazarquivir his army was wiped out and he himself killed. At the time it was not known that he was dead, and rumour persisted that he had been captured.

† The date given by Paez corresponds exactly with that in the Chronicle of Susenyos. The comet was also seen on 10 November and on 22 and 23 of that month by the ambassador to the court of the King of Persia, who has left a description of it. The *Historia Universalis Omnium Cometarum* by S. Lubienietski (1661) records the appearance of three comets in 1618, two of which were observed late that year. These comets were quite famous and formed the subject of a study by Kepler (*De Cometis, libelli tres*, 1619) and also of a published dispute at the Roman College between Fr. Orazio Grassi, professor of mathematics there, and Galileo: *De Tribus Cometis Anni MDCXVIII: Disputatio Astronomica* (1619).

with his son Fasiladas, then a youth of eighteen, and for the three following days both gave a hand in the building. It was another two years before the church was ready for worship. Paez wrote:

> It is all built of cantaria. It is small, seventy-two palms long and twenty-eight broad, but that is only the main body of the church. There is also a detached chapel thirty-two palms long and twenty-four wide. The chapel and sacristy are built of good reddish stone, the church itself of white stone, very well carved. The façade and side doors are decorated with eight columns, the capitals, bases and frieze so well carved that everyone who has seen them says it is not a work done on earth but in heaven. There is a choir with very fine wood carvings and a font for baptism and two others for holy water, all three of them also elegantly chiselled. On both sides there are windows with ornamental roses on the outside. In the centre of the front colonnade is a most attractive cross the base of which is carved like lace, and on the right of the front elevation a tower with a copper bell which we obtained from India.

An interior staircase in this tower led to a terraced roof, which gave a distant view southward to the mountains of Gojjam and eastward to Begameder. Dedicated to the Blessed Virgin under the title of Mariam Gimb or St Mary's Stone Building, perhaps as an indication to Ethiopians that Rome also honoured Our Lady, it was situated some three hours' mule trek from Gorgora on a wooded promontory of Lake Tana and was bounded by a deep creek frequented by hippopotamuses. One wall of the nave is still standing with its ornate carvings intact. Formerly it supported a barrel roof which can be seen only above the choir. The modest dimensions of the church would indicate that any mass conversion of the country to Rome was still remote from Paez's thinking.

In these years, while supervising the building of the church at Gorgora, Paez was engaged also in writing his *History of Ethiopia*. He had been asked to undertake this task by his Superiors in Goa and Rome in order to refute the false ideas about the country that were circulating in Europe thanks mainly to the writings of the Dominican friar Luis Urreta, whose popular *Historia de la Ethiopia* had been published in 1610 at Valencia. 'The Superiors in India,' writes Almeida, 'sent him what Frei Luis Urreta had published a little while before so that he should refute the great number of errors and lies that Ioão Balthazar had put into the author's head.'

This Balthazar, from whom Urreta had got his information, was an Ethiopian nobleman who claimed direct descent from one of the three Magi who bore the same name. Relying on this source Urreta states that the Emperors were ordained priests and, being celibate, were unable to add to the number of claimants to the throne; he held also that the word 'Abyssinia' meant an unconquered kingdom, and that the Alps and Pyrenees would look like 'lowly huts' by comparison with the mountains at the source of the Nile. Speaking of the 'immense riches' of the country he made the absurd statemeant that after the rainfalls the ground shone with gold washed up by the water. Urreta was not the only one who, having never visited Ethiopia, presumed to contradict the Jesuit missionaries.

To carry conviction Paez is careful to include his source for every statement not based on his own observation. From a scientific viewpoint, it is thoroughly satisfactory work. The legend of the Queen of Sheba he retails from the *Kebra Nagast* or *Glory of the Kings*, which he had found at Aksum, where he also had seen the Book of Ceremonies for the coronation of Emperors. He distinguishes between books he has read himself, like *Rites and Prayers for the Initiation of Monks*, and those he has not been permitted to see but which have been described to him by others; among these were the *Life of the Abbot Stateus* and the Ritual for Conferring Holy Orders. Among living authorities he cites certain men at court, or the Superior of a monastery, or state officials, or Gabriel the Portuguese. Much of his information he gathered directly from the Emperor, Cela Krestos and the Imperial Treasurer: to the first two he was indebted for the paragraphs on the alleged treasures on the amba Guexen, the method of electing an emperor, and on the course of the Nile, while the Treasurer gave him details of taxes and tributes.*

This extremely detailed reference to his sources makes Paez's *History* a work of unique value. Almeida's larger book (he takes the story of the Jesuits as far as 1634) is based – with the exception, of course, of the last section – on Paez, as he explained in a letter to Fr. Vitelleschi in 1639:

> As a Castilian, Paez had not a perfect command of the Portuguese language in which he wrote: he had forgotten Spanish, not having used it for many years, though often using Arabic, Turkish, Amharic

* Cf. Appendix 2.

130

and the other language [Ge'ez], the language of the books of Ethiopia, which he had learnt. For these reasons the Superior, who was then Fr. Antonio Fernandes, with the concurrence of the other Fathers at the assembly we held at Gorgora at the beginning of the year 1626, charged me to describe that Christian state for the service of God and in order to make it widely known.

At a time when Aristotle's was the only categorization of animals and plants, and natural history was an *a priori* quasi-science, Paez's description of the zebra, rhinoceros and leopard, though not so picturesque as Lobo's, are more exact than those found in contemporary writers. But with so much on hand both at court and at Gorgora, and with the frequent visits he made to the Portuguese, Paez was left with little time to polish his work. There are frequent repetitions, inconsistencies in spelling, imperfect ordering of his material, and Spanish words interspersed with Portuguese; however, these defects, which occur also in his letters to Iturén and in his reports to Rome, detract little from the value of the *History*. It was an astounding feat for an overworked man who perhaps considered it merely a draft. This effort to comply with orders from his Superiors may well have taxed Paez's health to a degree that left him with little resistance to the fever that was to cause his death.

It is not known when the Emperor received the letter of Paul V dated 25 November 1619, but it is unlikely to have reached him before the completion of the church of Gorgora. The Pope had clearly been kept informed by Fr. Vitelleschi of the difficulties facing Susenyos in his approach to Rome. He spoke of 'the incredible spiritual happiness' that the Emperor's letter, written two years earlier, had given him, and he praised his fortitude in facing the dangers he encountered daily in his zeal for the true faith. Echoing Paez's words of encouragement, the Pope reminded Susenyos that God always conquered in the end; this would happen again because the tumults in his country had been provoked by God's enemies.

On 16 January 1622 the church was dedicated by Paez. It was to be the last of his buildings. In March the Emperor, returning from Dancaz where he had been at the time of the dedication, called to see him at Gorgora. He now resolved to declare himself a Roman Catholic. That year he had won a decisive victory over his enemies. Regarding this as a sign of divine approval for his resolution, he sent for Paez and as proof of his sincerity put away all his wives except the first. Then making profession of the Roman faith he confessed and received the sacraments. On his return to Gorgora, Paez caught the fever that the Jesuits ascribed to the vapours rising from the scorched earth after the fall of the first showers. In July 1617 he had been close to death from an earlier attack, which had prevented him writing his annual letter to Thomas Iturén, the friend of his student days in Spain; it had left him sallow and gaunt. 'Having too much heated himself with zeal,' writes Bruce, 'he was taken with a violent fever on his arrival and though everything was done by Fr. Fernandes he died on 3 May 1622.'

The Emperor wrote a letter to the Provincial of Goa, speaking of 'the most penitent and virtuous Pedro Paez, our spiritual father, bright sun of the faith that cleared Ethiopia of the darkness of Eutyches'. In his classic *History of Ethiopia*, Sir Wallis Budge writes that Susenyos saw in him a

> deeply religious and learned man, whose body and brains were working at all times to spread the faith which he professed. He fasted and prayed, and toiled as hard at manual labour as the ordinary artisan of the country. He designed palaces and monasteries with excellent taste and he had made himself master of the trades of builder, mason, carpenter and blacksmith in the nineteen years of his life as missionary in Abyssinia. His humility and modesty were as great as his learning, and his cheerfulness and address were such that even those who hated his opinions loved the man.

Paez was buried in the old church at Gorgora. His remains were later transferred to the new church there, which was incomplete at the time of his death.

8

The death of Paez in 1622 left only five Jesuits in Ethiopia. Later the same year Fr. Antonio de Angelis died. He had been regarded as a saint by the people of Gojjam, who spoke of him always as 'the holy Father'. At the court of Cela Krestos he held a position similar to that of Paez at Dancaz; and it was said that Cela Krestos, whom he accompanied on his campaigns, would not charge the enemy until he had first bared and bowed his head and kissed the priest's hand. De Angelis had been in Ethiopia for eighteen years that had been 'full of hardships neither few nor slight'.

Before Paez's death Susenyos had written to the Jesuit General, Mutio Vitelleschi, requesting more priests, but the passage from Goa was now no safer than it had been when Paez and Monserrate set out for the country in 1589. Vitelleschi's reply was prompt. He wrote to Goa ordering a further twelve priests to be sent, naming three of whom one was to be his personal representative to thank the Emperor for his continued protection of the Roman Church and his favour shown to the missionaries.

On 28 November 1622, Emmanuel de Almeida, Vitelleschi's envoy, left Goa with two other Fathers in a *paguel*, a south Indian cargo boat, and almost suffered the same fate as Paez did in 1589. However, as Almeida himself wrote, they were fortunate to escape 'dangers from storms, from pirates, English and Dutch, Moors from Dhofar, and from the galleys and gelvas of the Turks' off the coast of Shihr and Aden. From 18 May to 16 October they were becalmed in the Bay of Dhofar in daily danger of discovery by boarding parties from the ruler of Qishn. Whenever men from the mainland came on board, the Jesuits were hidden in the hold of the vessel and in consequence contracted scabies. Eventually they reached Massawa on 24 January 1624. From there they went to the village of Zabot, five miles south-east of Asmara, which the Emperor had given the Jesuits to facilitate the reception of alms from India. At the time, Keba Krestos, a kinsman of the Emperor, was encamped near Debaroa, and he sent an escort to see the Fathers safe to Fremona. There they were welcomed by Fr. Didaco de Mattos, a Jesuit from Coimbra who had arrived in Ethiopia in 1620.

In a letter reporting their safe arrival Fr. Emmanuel Barradas, one of the party, spoke of the high reputation of the Jesuits in the country, but pointed out that the mission was in financial difficulties. He suggested that since no help could be expected from the Viceroy owing to the pressing needs of India, some of the funds of the Mogul mission, which was comparatively well established, might be directed to Ethiopia; he asked also that only the 'best men' be sent, a plea reiterated in the same mail by Fernandes, who wrote: 'Priests sent to Ethiopia should be persons of great prudence selected with the utmost care, for any display of immoderate zeal would cause the collapse of the edifice so painstakingly constructed.'

The remaining priests detailed for Ethiopia were to be sent by different routes lest they should all fall captive to the Turks together. At the instance of Philip III, the Viceroy of India had been enquiring into the feasibility of entering the country via the kingdom of Monomotapa, north of the Zambesi, and Lake Masura, now Lake Nyasa. The Jesuits in Mozambique reported in 1624 that it was impracticable: the distance from Tete to Tana was calculated to be some 4,600 miles, the natives were said to be fierce and provisions uncertain; the route was 'neither short, suitable nor safe'. Entry via Cairo was also considered but rejected as less safe than the sea approach via Suakin. Little definite information could be gathered concerning the trail via Melinde but, since the Governor of Mombasa had promised his assistance, the Viceroy decided that two Fathers should be sent by this route, which Fernandes had attempted in reverse ten years earlier. It was believed that because the Ethiopians traded with the Portuguese on the east coast of Africa there would be no difficulty in finding guides there to conduct the priests to the interior. Two other Fathers were to go via Zeila, a route mentioned in Susenyos's letter to Vitelleschi, though it seems that a scribe had written 'Zeila', on the Somali coast, instead of 'Dankal', the name given to the lowlands of Eritrea from the Hawash to the Gulf of Zula.

Jeronimo Lobo and his companion, Juan de Velasco, were chosen for Melinde, while Francisco Machado, a professor of theology at St Paul's seminary in Goa, and Bernardo Pereira, a recently ordained priest, were to try to enter the country via Zeila. Lobo's adventures had begun shortly after leaving Lisbon on 29 April 1621. The convoy in which he sailed was becalmed near the Line, where several hundred died of scurvy and the ships were forced to return to Portugal. He set out again on 18 March 1622 with the newly appointed Viceroy, Dom Francisco da Gama. Near Mozambique the five Portuguese ships forming the convoy were attacked by three Dutch and three British privateers. The Viceroy's ship, with Lobo and an incompetent pilot on board, ran aground in Mozambique and was seized. After three months some small boats were fitted out in which the stranded men proposed to cross to Goa: the largest vessel, in addition to sails, carried twenty-eight oarsmen. All the ships were scattered in a storm. The Viceroy, with Lobo, put back to Mozambique and on a second attempt made Cochin. Goa was reached on 16 December 1622. Lobo stayed there a year, setting out for Melinde on 26 January 1624.

Lobo gives a vivid account of his adventures in the country to the south-west of Ethiopia. He took with him a complete Turkish outfit, a shirt with flowing sleeves, a jacket and wide trousers fastened at the ankle and a large turban. He could also if necessary, dress as an Arab or as a Portuguese. From Ampaza, which the Fathers reached without incident, they went to the island of Pate, where they decided it would be better if only one made the initial attempt. Velasco stayed behind, while Lobo, with a Portuguese he does not name, set out northward along the Somali coast, climbing rocks, wading through quicksand, carrying provisions and water on his back and, on one occasion, firing his musket into the air to drive off an assault by tribesmen. As no one was able or dared to guide them inland, Lobo realized he was labouring in vain, returned to his companion and with him sailed for Diu. On his way back he caught fever. He was treated by an Arab doctor who, as he writes, 'came into my room, holding in his hand a mallet, a sort of dagger covered with rust and three horned leeches which were nearly half a foot long'.

Machado and Pereira, both about thirty-eight years old, made their way to Qishn dressed as Arabs and landed safely on 15 March 1624. From there Machado wrote to say that they had been invited to dinner by the Governor, who sent a message to the Moorish king of Adal seeking permission for the Fathers to proceed to Zeila. This the king readily granted and had his own cutter manned so that the Fathers should not fall into the hands of the Turks on their way up the coast. From Zeila Machado sent a letter to the Provincial at Goa, saying the voyage had been uncomfortable but once more they had been well received on their arrival by the Governor in the absence of the king at Auca Guriel, probably the modern Aussa in the district of Harar, which had been Grañ's base of operations. Letters came from the king ordering the priests to his presence. Pereira describes the commerce of Zeila and how he and Machado took to the road with a large number of sailors and merchants. Over a year later Almeida learnt that the Moorish king had sent a servant to behead the two Jesuits in the house where they had been lodged. 'Human witnesses there were not, for the savage [king] willed that only the public executioner, at night, in the dark and where they were, should carry out the cruel sentence he had pronounced against the saints.'

While waiting at Fremona, as Paez had done in 1604, for a summons to court, Almeida and his companions began their apostolate. In Tigre, wrote Almeida, 'many doors are opening to our preaching and to the acceptance of the Roman faith'. This was also the judgement of the veteran Antonio Fernandes. In a letter dated 18 February 1624, after reporting the safe arrival of Almeida, he spoke of the Church as 'prospering'. He had been teaching the Ethiopian clergy the 'correct manner of offering Mass' and had also amended their liturgical books; since he adjudged Ethiopian marriages invalid because they allowed the possibility of divorce, he had arranged for an imperial decree to be promulgated depriving lay judges of their power to dissolve marriages. Writing six weeks later, his companion Aloysius de Azevedo was equally optimistic: 'almost all the chiefs, priests and monks with an innumerable multitude of people' now professed the Roman faith and were waiting excitedly for the arrival of the new Patriarch. The Emperor, on the other hand, had reservations. In a letter to Urban VIII dated 2 May 1624 he explained that, while the greater number of his people favoured Catholicism, there were some violently opposed to it who were busy working among the populace to persuade them to hold doggedly to 'the false faith of their fathers'.

When Almeida reached the palace at Dancaz built by Paez, the Emperor gave him a warm welcome. Hardened by long campaigning Susenyos was now an even more impressive figure than he had been in his youth – 'tall, with the features of a man of quality, large, handsome eyes, pointed nose and an ample and well-groomed beard'. Almeida kissed the Emperor's hand and greeted him in the name of the Jesuit General, who, as he said, had gone in the Emperor's name to prostrate himself at the feet of the Holy Father. He handed to Susenyos Fr. Vitelleschi's letter which Fernandes, now the Superior of the Jesuits in Ethiopia, interpreted.

The following day Almeida presented his gifts: a painting of the nativity from the Archbishop of Goa, a reliquary from the Portuguese Assistant General (the priest in the Jesuit curia responsible for the mission), an amber rosary, a coverlet embroidered in China from other Jesuit officials, and the prize gift, an organ, which one of Almeida's companions, Luis Cardeira, played; there was also a harp, a harpsichord and other musical instruments. Almeida was comforted by the devotion with which the Emperor received a crucifix placed in a rich casket made in China. After eight days at court the newly arrived Jesuits retired to Gorgora.

Almeida's next call was on Cela Krestos, still the Viceroy of Gojjam, to whom he also brought letters similar to those he had given the Emperor. On his return to Gorgora, Almeida devoted the winter to the study of Amharic and, on renouncing his office as Vitelleschi's envoy, went to live in Damot, south of the Abbai, where the Viceroy had asked for a Jesuit priest. In 1625 the new Patriarch arrived, Alfonso Mendes, the first to visit Ethiopia since Oviedo.

Alfonso Mendes was a native of Santo Alexio near Moura. He had taught rhetoric for five years at Coimbra before his ordination. Later he became professor of Scripture at the University of Evora and on the occasion of Philip IV's visit was chosen to preach before the monarch: his sermon, which was later printed, won favour with the King, who exercising his rights of *padroado* rewarded him in 1621 with the appointment to the Patriarchate of Ethiopia.*

Mendes was the choice neither of the Jesuit General, who was not consulted, nor of Urban VIII, who was informed of it by Mendes himself in a letter dated 1 May 1622, asking the Pope for the fullest faculties, commendatory letters to the Emperor and the pallium. His letters reveal his attachment to the kind of pomp that St Ignatius

* 'Oratio Habita Philippi III Hispanarum Regi Lusitaniae II in Academia Ebis-ensi', printed in A. Vasconcelles, S.J., *Anacephaeoses* (1621), 589-96.

had urged the first Patriarch to shun. Mendes argued, however that since the Pope had betrothed him to his Ethiopian bride he should also see that the same bride was provided with a dowry of befitting ornaments or, more specifically, with vestments from the Pope's private chapel so that he could celebrate the divine offices with some measure of majesty among 'an uncultivated people'. There may well have been some hesitation in Rome, for the appointment was not confirmed until 19 December that year. 'The Catholic King,' Mendes had told Vitelleschi, 'has designated me Patriarch of Ethiopia, and I cannot refuse.' It would seem that Urban VIII rejected his requests for vestments from the papal wardrobe, for on 18 February 1623 Mendes wrote asking Philip IV to arrange for their purchase from the proceeds of the *Bullae Cruciatae*;* he proposed also that the stipend allotted to the Patriarch should be paid anually not by the Viceroy of India, whose business it was to provide the missionaries with their annual pension, but by the King himself, whose greater resources made its payment more certain.

Mendes had asked also for two assistant bishops. He named Fr. Didaco Seco and another Jesuit, his own young secretary, João da Rocha, who although he had not yet completed his studies was engaged in assisting hm to edit his theological works. In a consistory held in Rome on 6 March 1623 the choice of Seco was confirmed, but da Rocha was to be consecrated only in the event of Seco's death. On 12 March Mendes was ordained Patriarch and Seco a bishop in the Jesuit church of San Roque. They sailed from Lisbon on the 20th and after wintering in Mozambique reached Goa on 28 May the following year, 1624. Mendes recounted in a letter to Europe the hardships of the voyage: storms, sickness and shipwrecks, and the death of Seco at sea. His arrival in Goa caused consternation. Against the advice of the Jesuit Provincial and his advisers, he staged a ceremonial entry into the city. Clothed in full pontificals, escorted by two or three gentlemen attendants and followed by da Rocha, not yet a bishop but decked out in the episcopal gear of the dead Seco, Mendes walked in solemn procession through the streets of

* The first *Bulla Cruciata* was granted by Urban II to the Counts of Barcelona in 1089. Others followed, granting indulgences and exemption from the laws of fasting to those engaged in war against the infidels; the alms from these Bulls were at first used exclusively to finance the wars but were later extended to a wide variety of ecclesiastical purposes.

Goa. This charade later led to the suspension of da Rocha, who already had given offence to the sailors on the voyage by his haughty conduct.

The Goa Jesuits had begged the Patriarch to enter the city like any other Father with no external pomp so that his arrival should not become known to the Turks. In anger the Jesuit Provincial there wrote to Rome: 'Now the news of his arrival is all over India and has certainly reached Suakin. Jesuit bishops in the missions should shun all show and arrogance as they have always done until now. In future it will be more satisfactory to appoint bishops from the men already in Ethiopia and not send them from Portugal.'

While still at Goa, Mendes complained to Vitelleschi that the Fathers there had unjustly accused him of drawing heavily on the scant resources of the mission to maintain the grandeur he judged fitting to his status. He also petitioned the Jesuit General to expedite with the Papacy the despatch of his pallium for himself and the mitre for da Rocha, who had been put out to grass in the Salsette peninsula. Finally he asked Vitelleschi to prevent the despatch of priests from other religious Orders to Ethiopia; the reason he gave was to 'avoid dissensions and controversies'.

In anticipation of the Patriarch's arrival the Emperor went to Aksum in 1624 with Cela Krestos and his two sons by his first wife, Fasiladas and Markos. There, in the cradle of Ethiopian Christianity, Susenyos issued a letter to all his people giving his reasons for becoming a Roman Catholic and stating the principal articles of his newly adopted creed in solemn phrases that matched the wording of Claudius's declaration of the Coptic faith in 1555. In outspoken language he denounced the criminal scandals of recent Abunas – Mark, Christodulus, Peter and Simon – leaving no one in doubt that the compelling reason for his conversion was the edifying lives of the Jesuit missionaries. He wrote:

> The Alexandrine Patriarchs, the successors of Dioscorus,* and the men sent by them to Ethiopia, persisted in restricting Christ to the possession of a single nature. Debilitated as they were by short rations of truth, they turned their back on righteousness to pursue paths unworthy of the lesser clergy, let alone bishops and patriarchs,

* Dioscorus (d. 454), Patriarch of Alexandria from 444, supported Eutyches, the true founder of monophysitism, but was deposed by the Council of Chalcedon in 451.

by shamelessly marrying and siring children, whose own children and grandchildren bear witness in Ethiopia to the lust of their fathers. And worse, they were in the habit of deflowering young marriageable girls as well as indulging in other unspeakable iniquities. They would offer to confer Holy Orders and consecrate altars in exchange for gold and salt bars, imposing their rapacious demands on ordinands, forcing them for six months or a whole year to carry water, wood or stone for the construction of their houses and enclosures, all this despite the fact that those guilty of such acts are liable to the condemnation of the Apostles written in the Book of Synods: 'Whoever gets ordained in exchange for payment is to be unfrocked and totally excommunicated together with the person who ordained him, just as Simon Magus was by Peter.'

The Emperor continued:

The Abuna Peter was convicted of the foulest possible crimes, unmentionable in polite society, for he put himself on a level with those who, lusting after other men's bodies, called down from heaven fire and sulphur. He came to a sticky end all right, since for his crimes he was stripped of his priesthood, imprisoned on the island of Dek,* and his stomach became extended to the size of a huge drum. The Abuna Christodulus was surrounded by troops of concubines, an affair notorious both to his contemporaries and to persons still alive.

After narrating the treachery of the Abuna Peter, who fully merited his death on the battlefield, Susenyos castigated Simon, who had caused such trouble to Paez.

The way was now made ready for the Patriarch from the West. Mendes, now in Bassein, where he picked up the stranded Lobo, wrote to the Jesuit General on 14 January 1624. He informed him that he had decided to go via Beilur, a small port some three hundred and twenty miles south of Massawa, against the advice of the Provincial, who favoured Suakin; he had sent the Provincial a sharp letter telling him that he was no longer bound to take the advice of Jesuit Superiors when he was a better judge of any issue himself. After the usual difficulties of finding a ship Mendes left Diu on 1 April 1625. He landed safely at Beilur and made his way through Danakil, a country he describes in his travel journal, the only important source for the history of the district at that period; this work,

* The larger of the two islands near the south end of Lake Tana.

incidentally, shows him to have been, like James Bruce, a brave and resourceful traveller with a self-esteem to match that of the laird. When eventually he came in sight of Fremona from the summit of the Senafe range he donned his archiepiscopal finery, strapped an ornate saddle onto his mule and on 21 June came down into the settlement amid the acclamations of the Portuguese. On 20 November he set out for court with a retinue of four priests, two Brothers, thirteen laymen, five musicians, two masons and two personal servants. Despite urgent pleas from the Emperor to hasten his arrival, Mendes appears to have delayed deliberately with the idea of creating an impression of importance on his leisurely progress through the countryside.

On 7 December he was at Ganeta Jesus, a small residence established by Paez in the neighbourhood of the Emperor's encampment. There he met a daughter of Susenyos and found her beautiful, 'more like a Portuguese than a native of these parts'. He then went on to Gorgora to await the return of the Emperor from a campaign in the north. While there he reordained twenty Ethiopian priests and monks, allowing those who had wives to keep them. It is not known whether it was his intention to insist on celibacy from new candidates. Mendes gave as his reason for this step the desire not to leave the parishes destitute of clergy, as though a parochial system comparable to that in Portugal existed in Ethiopia.

Eventually, on 7 February 1626, Mendes was summoned to court. Half a league from the camp he was met by 15,000 armed horsemen and accoutred gentlemen who made him a low bow and opening their ranks to the right and left took him between their lines, 'the air resounding with the noise of kettledrums, pipes and shouts'. At a tent a short distance from the camp he dismounted, put on his rochet and hat, and had 'all men kissing his hand'. He then proceeded to another tent where he donned a cope and white mitre, mounted a pied horse which was cloaked in white damask, and rode to the church of Gan Jabet under a canopy carried by six governors of provinces and some 'prime noblemen'. At the entrance to the church he was received by a discharge of all the cannon in the Emperor's armoury and some small shot. The *Benedictus* was then sung as he proceeded up the chancel where Susenyos, with a gold crown on his head, rose to embrace him.

Mendes's address to the assembly was a *tour de force*. As given in his own work, *Expeditio Aethiopica*, it comes to approximately

30,000 words; repeated through an interpreter, it must have lasted a very large part of the day. The speech was spattered with quotations from Aristotle, Tertullian, Eusebius and Jerome, and would have been an impressive display of erudition in any European university. However, it was hardly suitable for an audience whom he had dismissed as 'an uncultured people' in his first letter to the Pope after his appointment. In the central portion of the speech he demonstrated how the great sees of Antioch, Jerusalem, Constantinople and Alexandria had once been subject to Rome, which ultimately was responsible also for the introduction of Christianity into Ethiopia. The concluding section gave a history of the schism of Dioscorus and the attempts to heal it, especially at Florence; they had failed, but this last approach was about to be crowned with success. God speaking through the prophet Amos expressed Mendes's ambition: 'That day I shall re-erect the tottering house of David, make good the gaps in it, restore its ruins and rebuild it as it was in the days of old.'

There followed a solemn reception at court. Then a day was appointed, 11 February, for the Emperor and 'all the great men', clergy and laity, solemnly to swear obedience to the Church of Rome. The Emperor, holding the Bible, knelt before the Patriarch, took the oath of allegiance to the Pope, and was followed by the nobility and clergy. Mendes was still without an assistant bishop to add to the grandeur of the occasion. The Viceroy had written to Philip IV to say that da Rocha was unfit to be consecrated. He was soon proved correct, for shortly afterwards, as soon as he received an order to proceed to Ethiopia, the arrogant young Jesuit fled to the fortress of Muscat disguised as a soldier.

After his reception by the Emperor, Mendes made his first blundering proclamation: henceforth no clergy or monks were to offer Mass or perform any ecclesiastical function until they had first received faculties from himself. 'It was also ordered that all persons whatsoever should embrace the Roman faith under pain of death to such as should refuse and that none should presume to conceal those who did.' All the clergy were now to be reordained, churches reconsecrated, the faithful rebaptized, fasts and festivals rearranged according to the Tridentine calendar. Circumcision – which St Ignatius had listed among the practices to be allowed, at least temporarily – was prohibited, and the ancient liturgy was to be reformed. Overnight Mendes demanded that the Ethiopians should throw over the faith and practices they had cherished and defended for more than a thousand years. Virtually the entire population were to be treated as enemies of the crown.

Mendes could hardly have acted with greater folly. On his way from Fremona to court he had brushed aside as insignificant the manifest loathing for Roman Catholicism he had witnessed on his journey. Only the ingenuous Lobo mentions it: he speaks, for example, of the inhabitants of a certain village which greeted the Patriarch with 'one chorus of shrieks or lamentations'. Wherever he went he could not have failed to observe the fear manifested by the people, who believed that they were about to be ensnared in the false tenets of a foreign religion.

In 1624 Susenyos had already publicly declared his adhesion to Rome. Now Mendes's insistence on his repeating his submission in a grand manner before the entire court against the backdrop of the splendid hills of the heartland of Ethiopia was both unnecessary and provocative. It served only to enhance the sense of his own hollow achievement and self-importance, which was further inflated when the Emperor showered gifts on him: lands in Dambea, thirty-five oxen and 2,000 gold crowns; besides this one hundred oxen were sent to Fremona and two hundred more to Gorgora. In the months that followed more Jesuits entered the country. By 1628 there were nineteen priests in Ethiopia.

In Paez's eighteen years there the only direct mission to the people had been among the Agau. But Mendes now planned to force Roman Catholicism on all the provinces. It was particularly unfortunate for him that his arrival coincided with a very severe plague of locusts. This was at once interpreted as a visitation of God on the people for abandoning their ancient faith. Luckily the plague did not visit all the provinces in the same year. The people, moreover, knew twenty-four hours beforehand that the locusts were approaching, because the sun and earth appeared yellow with the shadow they cast, which was spread sometimes over twenty miles. Paez had observed that generally the devastation was greatest in the northern provinces, especially in Tigre. In 1626, the year of Mendes's arrival, the Fremona area was devastated – the disaster compounded, as it often was, by swarms of mice and monkeys. That year the Jesuit house was surrounded by peasants driven by starvation from their villages. The relief the Fathers could provide was insufficient to prevent the death of 'such numbers that their bodies filled the highways'; the hyenas, after devouring the carcases, fell on the living, sometimes so fiercely that they dragged children out from their homes. 'I saw myself,' writes Lobo, 'a troop of hyenas tear a child of six years old in pieces before I or anyone else could come to its assistance.' Tigre was almost 'unpeopled': men, women and children all left to find food in other provinces.

Lobo is as vivid as he is objective in his account of his experiences in trying to carry out Mendes's instructions. He illustrates both the heroism of the ordinary Jesuit priest at the time and the utter fatuity of the Patriarch's expectations.

In Tigre, Lobo's time was 'entirely taken up with the duties of the mission, preaching, confessing, baptising'. His first excursion was to a mountain village two days' journey from Fremona. The local chieftain was a Roman Catholic, his wife a bitter opponent of the Jesuits; she 'persuaded the inhabitants that the hosts we consecrated and gave to the communicants were mixed with juices strained from the flesh of a camel, a dog, a hare and a swine, all creatures which the Abyssinians look upon with abhorrence, believing them unclean'.

The inhabitants fled as Lobo and his companion carrying their Mass equipment were seen approaching. But the chief, who in the manner of a person of quality lived on the summit, received them with civility. His dependants had built their huts around his house, giving the impression that the settlement was much larger than in fact it was. On the priests' arrival he sent them the present of a cow, the customary token of regard. Several days were spent in conversation with the chieftain's wife but nothing was achieved. The priests then left for a more populated area. As they drew near they heard the same loud lamentations that had greeted Mendes on his journey south, as though the village had suffered a devastating calamity, and they were told the people had been warned against them as the devil's own missionaries who had come to seduce them from their old faith. None save the chieftain and the priest there received them into their homes. At a third village in the same district their lives were saved only through the intervention of the chieftain.

Back in the plain Lobo and his companion were at last successful. Here they were surrounded by such a multitude that the whole village was converted in a short time. This success was followed by another in the same neighbourhood. On this occasion they devised the procedure they subsequently followed, as Lobo records:

We erected our tents and placed our altar under some green trees for the benefit of the shade; and every day before sun-rising, my companion and I began to catechize and instruct these new Catholics. . . . When we were weary with speaking we placed in ranks those who were sufficiently instructed and passing through them with great vessels of water baptized them according to the form prescribed by the Church. As their number was very great we cried aloud, those in this rank are named Peter, those in that rank Anthony. And did the same among the women whom we separated from the men. We then confessed them and admitted them to communion. After Mass we applied ourselves to catechize, to instruct and to receive the renunciation of their errors, scarce allowing ourselves time to make a scanty meal, which we never did more than once a day.'

Later during this missionary journey a friendly Ethiopian explained to the Fathers the cause of the lamentations they had heard in the mountain villages. The people had been told by their priests and monks that the Jesuits, wherever they went, were followed by a cloud of locusts, a sign that they were men accursed by God. When no locusts followed their passage through this man's village he was convinced that the tale was a calumny. As Lobo pointed out, there were locusts in Ethiopia before any Jesuits came, and indeed before there were any Jesuits anywhere.

Lobo's narrative of his missionary experiences is supplemented by letters written to Rome by other priests. They list eminent Tigre converts and speak of the discovery of lime in the bed of the river Soleda, which facilitated the building of a new church at Fremona as well as a monument there to the Patriarch Oviedo. Bruno Bruni, a native of Civitella and a recent arrival, was in his own phrase the 'architect, builder and hewer of stone'. He had quickly won the affection of Susenyos, who had contributed generously to the building and its decoration. 'The Emperor,' Bruni wrote, 'sends me frequent and respectful letters when I am away; when I am with him he receives me as a son; when he sees me emaciated he grieves like a Father and enquires the reason; he asks what I am lacking and gives many other proofs of his fatherly love.' When Bruni was sent to reform the monastery at Dina the four hundred monks there held him in great honour. 'Their frequent tears made me weep,' he told Vitelleschi; 'quarrels which were endemic among them were composed, the practice of enclosure was restored, love of poverty and

145

chastity, almost dead among some of them, was revived.' It was perhaps significant also that his life was at times in danger. There was an occasion when a would-be assassin entered his church but, hearing him preach, threw aside his weapon, became a Catholic and the Father's friend.

Other letters describe the search for the body of Cristovão da Gama with a view to introducing his cause of beatification as the first Roman saint of Ethiopia. From Fremona one of the Fathers, Thomé Barneto, set out in 1627 for Goa to raise money for the mission, taking with him six Ethiopian youths to follow courses of higher studies at St Paul's College. In the south Almeida reported in June 1628 a reform of morals at court: judges had been appointed for matrimonial cases, a number of monks hitherto opposed to Catholicism had been won over, almost the entire winter was spent elucidating Scripture. The Emperor had attended Holy Week services at Ganeta Jesus the previous year and later had been present at the solemn dedication of Paez's church at Gorgora, making gifts of money, carpets and land to the Fathers; on that occasion the boys in the school had mounted a play to the amazement of the court.

However, throughout the country the Jesuits were more often shunned as heretics because they were thought not to honour the Virgin Mary. In Ethiopia a day was set aside each month to commemorate the Assumption and it was part of their belief that no Christians apart from themselves had a true sense of the greatness of the mother of God or paid her the honours she merited. Her good name was so protected that in some districts an oath taken in the name of the Virgin Mary, along with that of St George, was penalized with forfeiture of goods and even at times with the loss of life. When later the Jesuits were heard speaking of Mary with respect, the Ethiopians were prepared to give them credit for not being totally second-class Christians. These 'prepossessions', as Lobo calls them, more than any subtle divergences of doctrine were seen by the Jesuits as the main obstacle in the way of reuniting the Church of Ethiopia with Rome.

Not later than 1629, perhaps earlier, a letter from Pope Urban VIII, dated 1 February 1627, should have reached Dancaz – though it may well have been lost since the Jesuits make no mention of it. The scribes of the papal curia would seem to have been inspired by the style of the Ethiopian court writers: the Pope speaks of 'the torrent of the river Nile bringing joy to the city of God' and of 'fruits worthy of angelic banquets being borne from the parched plains of Ethiopia to the throne of St Peter'. The Pope congratulated Susenyos on manifesting 'a spirit worthy of your Davidic lineage in which the ruling house of Ethiopia is said to glory'. In a later letter to Fasiladas, Urban VIII expressed happiness at hearing that he had been designated to succeed the Emperor, exhorted him to follow in his father's footsteps and praised him for his zeal in promoting the frequent reception of the sacraments.

The kind of teaching given by Lobo and his fellow priests is indicated in an Ethiopian catechism printed in Rome in 1631 by the Congregation of Propaganda. Entitled *Alphabeticum Aethiopicum sive Abyssinum* it contains the Pater Noster, the Creed, Angelus and Ten Commandments in both Latin and Amharic characters, along with a rough guide to pronunciation. The small book also prints a transcription of the prologue of St John's gospel as far as the fourteenth verse (*et habitavit in nobis*), which when recited was presumably taken as acceptance of the dogma that there were two natures in Christ. The last pages give the numerals in Amharic, probably an aid to the Fathers in hearing confessions according to the Roman practice of enumerating sins. Later the Congregation of Propaganda drew up a new and fuller profession of faith that meant almost nothing to all but a handful of Ethiopians. It was a document of twelve or thirteen thousand words which included the dogmatic statements of the Council of Chalcedon and the Tridentine definitions of the sacrifice of the Mass; it also condemned the custom of deferring baptism for forty days that from the beginning of the mission had caused distress to the Jesuits.

With da Rocha out of the way, a new assistant bishop, Apollinaris de Almeida, was appointed. He had first sailed from Lisbon in 1626 and been forced back by bad weather; he had sailed again the following year, had been detained by lack of winds in the Red Sea island of Kamaran off south Yemen, and did not reach Fremona until August 1630. This was just thirteen months after Mendes wrote to Rome to acknowledge the receipt of the pallium he had coveted and first requested from the Pope in the letter announcing his appointment seven years earlier. It did nothing to diminish Mendes's self-importance when, in September 1630 wearing the pallium, he was ceremoniously received by Susenyos to deliver to him letters of credence from Urban VIII and Philip IV, brought by the assistant bishop.

The newly established Congregation of Propaganda was, it

seems, attempting to legislate for a situation that hardly corresponded with conditions in Ethiopia. In 1630, for instance, Mendes was ordered to consult the Pope with a view to obtaining a licence to establish a university or *academia generalis* in the country; there was also to be an Amharic press to be managed by three or four Ethiopian Brothers, though none in fact had been admitted into the Society.

Mendes, for his part, appears to have shown no appreciation of the praiseworthy practices of the Ethiopian Christians. They received the Sacraments more frequently than was the custom in the West, fasted more severely, and behaved with greater decorum in church.* Nor did Mendes understand how in the recent struggle against Islam their faith had become even more closely identified with their nationhood. The Patriarch presumed that the principle *cujus regio ejus religio* held in Africa as it did in Europe. With the Emperor behind him he saw no reason why Roman Catholicism should not be imposed on the entire country, and took no notice of the unease of the Ethiopians when they saw new stations of the Jesuits established in the provinces.

The nineteen priests were now scattered in eleven places: at Gorgora and Ganeta Jesus, some twenty miles from Dancaz, at Nebesse, Adaza, Saria and Collela in Gojjam; at Fremona and Debaroa in Tigre; and also in Agaumeder and Begameder. With them were a number of Brothers and various assistants. Lands had been given them for schools and seminaries, and the foundation of a cathedral befitting the new Patriarch had been laid. All this alone was enough to cause alarm, but Mendes nevertheless demanded more priests. Thanks to his ostentatious behaviour in Goa the route to Fremona via Massawa was now permanently closed. Other ways of entry were desperately explored. On 25 March 1628 the French consul in Cairo reported the fate of four Italians: on their arrival in Egypt he had sent them over three hundred and twenty miles up the Nile to another French consul at Girge, who had promised to see

---

* The reverence shown by the faithful in their churches impressed later travellers. The Frenchman, Poncet, in the eighteenth century, wrote that the Ethiopians showed much more awe and modesty in their churches than the Europeans generally did. They entered bare-footed, moved silently on the carpeted floor, and were clothed always in clean linen. 'No one,' he observed, 'is heard to speak or blow his nose or turn his head.'

them safely into Ethiopia. But a Greek merchant from Kos had delated them as 'Spanish spies' to the pasha, who ordered them back to Cairo. After several months' imprisonment the consul raised money for their ransom and wrote to Vitelleschi asking to be refunded. As late as 1630 another two priests set out from Luanda in Angola: the Rector of the Jesuit college there had reported to Rome that the 'King of Congo', who previously had held the Portuguese in suspicion, had encouraged the Jesuits to attempt that route, stating that 40,000 Ethiopians, nominally Christians, lived on the borders of his country.*

It was prudence more than men that was needed, however, as the veteran Fernandes had pointed out. Almeida, who had now succeeded as Superior, added in a letter of June 1628 that no more men should be sent since the mission was unable to support them. Funds had not arrived from India in answer to his pressing request, and no more lands could be asked for from the Emperor because their cultivation required a large outlay and would also render the Fathers open to the charge of avarice. But all the time Mendes himself remained unaware of the swelling opposition to the Roman faith. Only the Fathers scattered now throughout the provinces were alert to the deep-seated enmity to Rome.

Lobo gives a truer assessment of the situation than does Mendes in his long and frequent reports to Propaganda. After serving the mountain mission for two years in Tigre, Lobo was transferred to Limgenes in Damot, which he found 'one of the most beautiful and agreeable places in the world. . . . The whole region seemed a garden laid out and cultivated to give pleasure. ' He doubted whether even 'the imagination of a painter had yet conceived a landscape as beautiful', and there he built a church of hewn stone roofed and wainscoted with cedar. Lobo found the people 'inflexibly obstinate', and illustrated this with an incident that has parallels in Ethiopian history: 'When I first published the Emperor's edict that required all his subjects to renounce their errors and unite themselves with the Roman Church, there were some monks who, to the

---

* Soon after the Portuguese discovered the kingdom of Congo in 1481 its rulers adopted Christianity. One of them, Dom Affonso I, who ruled from 1506 to 1545, became an excellent Christian and sent some noble Congolese youths to Lisbon for their education. With the early missionaries came blacksmiths, bricklayers and other skilled labourers.

number sixty, chose rather to die by throwing themselves headlong over a precipice than to obey their sovereign's command.'

During this time the Jesuits met each year after celebrating Christmas in their own stations; their purpose was both to 'comfort and entertain each other' and to 'relate the progress of our missions and concert all measures that might further the conversion of the inhabitants'. On one such occasion in the neighbourhood of the imperial camp on the last stage of their journey, the house they were lodged in was barricaded at nightfall and fired by a train attached to its thatched roof. Fortunately one door was left unfastened and the priests made their escape. 'The measures were so well laid,' writes Lobo, 'that the house was in ashes in an instant.' There is no report of the subjects discussed at these meetings, which Mendes did not attend.

In 1628 a rebellion broke out among the Agua. The Emperor marched against them and was repulsed when he assaulted their defensive trenches, but Cela Krestos answered his brother's call for help and won some engagements in the open plain. A more specifically religious rising was led the next year in Tigre by the Viceroy, who abandoned the Catholic faith he had adopted a few years earlier. Mendes admitted that it halted the progress made in the previous year. But he failed to read the portents, being content to tell the Pope that the Emperor had given not only money but his crown of gold to the cathedral which, when completed, would be a striking monument to the new faith.

In 1630 Sarsa Krestos, the Viceroy of Begameder and nephew of Susenyos, rose against the Emperor. He carried off the chief courtiers, declared himself the defender of the Alexandrine faith and proclaimed Fasiladas Emperor. He also made mischief between Susenyos and Cela Krestos, who was falsely charged with complicity. Within the year, deserted by his troops, Sarsa Krestos, fled, only to be brought half-naked and weighed down with boulders before the Emperor. Susenyos ordered him to be hanged privately. Next it was the turn of the Governor of Shoa. As it became clear that people in many parts of the country were rejecting Roman Catholicism, Mendes made his greatest blunder of all: he pressed the Emperor to impose Catholicism by force. Takla Giyorgis, the Emperor's son-in-law, protested vehemently, seized his convert military chaplain, the Abbot Jacobo, killed him, and burned his crucifix and Roman missals. He too then rebelled, was taken prisoner and hanged. Laka Maryam, a high-ranking officer in Begameder, was thrown over a precipice when he revolted.

More grave was the rising of Malka Krestos, the Emperor's brother. On 27 June 1632 scouts brought Susenyos news that his force of 25,000, many of them ill-armed, were marching against him. At noon the two armies came in sight of each other. Then the Emperor

> clapped spurs to his horse, and being followed by the cavalry, won a complete victory at the first charge, the peasants flying like so many sheep before the wolves. The night coming on saved many of those wretches, though others were beaten to pieces, casting themselves down precipices. The pursuit continued till late, when the Imperialists made themselves master of their camp.

The next day the slain numbered eight thousand. As Fasiladas pointed out, these were neither pagans nor Muslims, but the Emperor's 'own subjects and countrymen, and some of them his relatives'. Mendes, in a letter to the Pope, places the blame for the aftermath of the battle squarely on the

> disturbers of the peace who took the Emperor aside and showed him the fields strewn with corpses. 'Look,' they said, 'not one of these men whose bones cover the earth is a foreigner; there is not one of us but has lost a brother or a son or someone bound to us by ties of blood. Whether we are vanquished or whether we vanquish, it is the same, we are the losers. It is five years since we did not have arms in our hands; we have neither time nor strength on our side; we can find no men to cut the hay for the horses or guard the mules or bear arms. The cause of our plight is the name of the Roman faith. . . . If you do not permit these peasants and ignorant people their ancient customs, the kingdom is lost to you and your posterity.'

Mendes says the Emperor was shaken by these words. His very victories added to the bitterness and disillusionment of his supporters. To satisfy hostile clamours he asked Mendes to make three concessions; namely, the restoration of the ancient liturgy of the Mass, the return to Wednesday from Saturday fasting, and the celebration of feasts according to the Ethiopian calendar. In 1629 Mendes agreed. Meanwhile taking advantage of the Emperor's embarrassment the Galla again invaded Gojjam. Then Susenyos was asked to allow the people to choose their own Church, Ethiopian or Roman. On 24 June 1632 the Emperor granted this despite Mendes's protests. 'It would be too tedious to mention all the differences and controversies between the Emperor and the Patriarch, and therefore we must pass them over as not material to our purpose,' writes Almeida. Let those who accepted the Roman faith, the proclamation ran, 'remain in it, as the Portuguese had done in the time of Sarsa Dengel; let each have their own altars and their own liturgy'.

Old and worn out by war and sickness, as he himself wrote, and no longer capable of governing, Susenyos handed over power to his son Fasiladas as he had promised to do on his last battlefield. The Ethiopian Chronicle records the reaction of the people:

> The whole camp as if they had some great deliverance from the enemy rang with shouts and acclamations. The monks and clergy who had felt the greater weight of the Fathers' hatred lifted up their thankful voices to heaven. The promiscuous multitude of men and women danced and capered. . . . They broke to pieces their own rosaries and those of all whom they met. . . . Others ran about singing for joy . . . chanting forth the following lines:

> *At length the sheep of Ethiopia freed*
> *From the bad lions of the West*
> *Securely in their pastures feed.*
> *St Mark and Cyril's doctrines have overcome*
> *The follies of the Church of Rome.*

A few days after the publication of the edict, 'there was a general circumcision, followed by a universal baptism after their former manner, after which they judged themselves free of the obligation of being tied to one wife, and publicly declared that for the future they would marry and remarry as they pleased.'

Mendes was absent from court and received the news with fury. There was yet another rebellion led by Sarsa Krestos, Viceroy of Gojjam, in which Fasiladas played a dubious role. Susenyos lived on another three months, dying on 7 September 1632 at the age of sixty-one in the twenty-fifth year of his reign. On his deathbed he again professed his allegiance to the faith of Rome, declaring that he had granted his people freedom to choose their religion in order to prevent further bloodshed and yet more risings provoked by turbulent monks. A brave, wise and prudent man, he ended his days in sadness: his deep Christian piety had led him to put his trust in Mendes rather than in his own political good sense. As Wallis Budge points out, the cause of his undoing was the support he gave to Mendes's ambition to achieve immediately the conversion of the whole country to the Roman Church. 'That he clung to the new faith which he embraced to the day of his death,' writes Budge,* 'and abdicated when he found that he had ceased to be the king desired by his people, show that he was a man who possessed high ideals.'

Susenyos was attended on his deathbed by Fr. Didaco de Mattos, who had been with him in his campaign against the Agau and at one time had explained the gospel of St Matthew in the residence of Prince Fasiladas. Mattos's last assignment had been on the island of Dek in Lake Tana, where many kings and princes were buried; at the request of the Emperor he had undertaken the reform of the numerous monasteries there.

Great pomp surrounded the burial in the church of Ganeta Jesus that the Emperor had built. Almeida, who was present, describes the scene:

An Egyptian made the bier with small steps, almost square, onto which they placed the body wrapped in buckram, covering it with a large piece of taffeta of several colours. Before this bier were carried the imperial colours. . . . Alongside them went the kettledrums, beating at times a melancholy tone; then two or three of the best horses he used to ride with their richest furniture; next several pages and other servants carrying parts of his imperial robes and ornaments, one his vest, another his sword, a third his crown and so others his sash, his beads, his javelin, his target. These things divers persons took by turns, showing them to excite tears and sighs. . . . The Queen, his daughters and all the ladies of the court rode on mules, their hair cut off and a slip of fine white cloth, two inches broad, tied about their heads, the end hanging behind. All the company was in their mourning, which consisted of any old rag, but those who would express it most put on black leather or cloth and clipped their heads. There was no sort of light carried nor any in the church but there was much weeping until he was buried.

* *A History of Ethiopia*, Vol. 2, 396.

Epilogue

From the first day of his reign Fasiladas, Susenyos's eldest son, made clear his religious stand. When the Jesuits came to congratulate him on his accession, he refused to see them or even allow them to remain at court. After depriving them of their lands and the firearms they had been permittd to carry on their travels, he ordered them first to Collela, then to Fremona. As they made their way north they were robbed by their own escort and, had not the intrepid Lobo brought up a party of Portuguese to meet them, they might well have been murdered in the mountains.

From Fremona on 24 April 1633 Mendes sent Fasiladas a letter of remonstrance. In reply the Emperor recalled how, after the last battle fought by Susenyos, 'the learned and unlearned, clergy and laity, civil and military, young and old, all sorts of persons had addressed my father, crying out . . . "How long shall we thrust our swords into our own bowels?"' Then continuing, he complained about the reiteration of baptism as if his people had been heathens: 'They reordained our priests and deacons, they burned the wooden chests of our altars and consecrated altars of their own as if ours had not been consecrated before.' Mendes was ready for concessions, but it was too late. Nothing of Paez's laborious achievement could now be salvaged.

In an attempt two months later to restore his position, Mendes despatched to Goa four priests under Almeida with instructions to arrange for Portuguese troops to be sent against Falsiladas. Since the party had no passes from the Emperor they took a circuitous route to the coast, which they reached near Defalo, ten leagues south from Massawa; here 'the sun scorched the sands like fire' so that the ground on which they lay was 'as hot as a hearth'. At Aden, where their ship put in after being dismasted in a storm, the priests were held for six months while a ransom was arranged. Eventually they reached Diu in September 1634. Shortly afterwards a Portuguese naval force attacked Mombasa. Fasiladas, believing this was a run-up to an assault on Ethiopia, ordered Mendes and all Jesuits out of the country, but the Patriarch was not so easily exiled. He remained at Fremona with nine others until Fasiladas sent to have him forcibly removed. Never lacking courage, Mendes slipped out of Fremona and sought the protection of the Ethiopian governor of the sea coast province of Serae, who had rebelled and not yet made his formal submission to the Emperor. First the governor sent them for safety to an amba, the summit of which contained a small village with 'thatched cottages more like the dens of wild beasts than the habitations of men'. Mendes's plan seems to have been to make the province the base of operations for the Portuguese forces he had requested from Goa.

When the Governor was offered a free pardon in exchange for Mendes's person, he compromised by delivering him instead to the Turks at Arquico, the mainland fort that provided fresh water for Massawa. The Turkish commander there, when he was told that the priests were taking out gold, stripped them; he found only two silver chalices and some coins which 'would keep them but a few days with good husbandry'. From Arquico, Mendes wrote a vitriolic letter to the Emperor accusing him of mendacity and deceit. Later the prisoners were sent to Suakin, where the pasha was restrained from killing them only when he was informed that, if he did, he would lose his trade with Diu. Instead he demanded a large ransom which was paid after several months.

Mendes's humiliation was complete when, during his imprisonment, the Coptic Patriarch sent from Cairo to replace him passed through the port on his way to Ethiopia. His arrival is recorded tersely in the Ethiopian Chronicle: 'That year, there arrived the Patriarch with the holy ark. His name was Rezeq. . . . The Frank Alfonso [Mendes] returned to his own country.'

Mendes was now held back with two priests. The other seven in his party sailed for India, commissioned by him to put to the Viceroy his plan for four hundred Portuguese troops to be despatched to the Red Sea in order to seize Suakin, Massawa and Arquico, capture the trade of these ports, then bring pressure on the Emperor to restore the Jesuit mission. The Viceroy did not respond. Nevertheless when Mendes himself reached India he continued to solicit

155

military help. 'The methods that he proposed to preserve and extend our religion,' wrote a fellow Jesuit, 'were more those of a conqueror than of a missionary and a bishop. He said it was necessary . . . to dethrone the Emperor and replace him by his brother and then provoke civil war in Abyssinia.' Lobo, who criticizes Mendes in similar terms, was charged by the Patriarch to explain this invasion plans to Rome. On leaving Goa he was shipwrecked south of the coast of Natal, near the Umzimvubu river. After rounding the Cape to Angola, he found a ship to take him to Cartagena. Then he was captured by pirates and marooned on a deserted island from which he escaped in a small boat. By stages Lobo made his way to Lisbon, arriving on 8 December 1636. In Rome 'the Pope [Urban VIII], the Cardinals and all those who heard him came to believe that the missionaries had introduced into their speech and all their conduct something of that martial temper only too natural to the Portuguese.'

Nothing came of Lobo's mission. Portugal was distracted from her interests overseas by her domestic struggle for independence from Spain, which she obtained in 1640. That year Mendes's assistant bishop, Apollinaris de Almeida, who with seven Fathers had insisted on remaining in Ethiopia, was hanged with five of them 'in a town where a fair was kept that day and . . . in sight of a multitude of people'; the other two had previously been assassinated. Mendes remained in Goa where he died in 1656 at the age of seventy-six.

The Portuguese enterprise in Ethiopia had begun with da Gama's chivalrous campaign which saved the country from Islam. Oviedo's approach had been intolerant. Paez, broadminded, diplomatic, sincere, painstaking and faithful to the instructions of St Ignatius, came close to success, only to have his achievement thrown away by the blundering arrogance of Mendes.

A short time later French and Italian Capuchins sought to enter the country. They got no further than the coast, where they were murdered. Their heads and skins, stuffed with dried grass, were sent by the Muslim ruler to Fasiladas to emphasize his enforcement of a treaty by which he undertook to allow no foreigners into the country. Their blood sealed off Ethiopia from the West for the next century and a half. Gibbon was all but justified in writing: 'The Gates of that solitary realm were for ever shut against the arts, the science and the fanaticism of Europe.' Fasiladas had twenty-four brothers and half-brothers, for Susenyos before his conversion had many wives and concubines: every one of these brothers he afterwards put to death, and then fell to persecuting Ethiopians who professed the Roman faith. Cela Krestos, deprived of his lands, but loyal to the Pope, was exiled to the mountains of Semen. Several priests who had been ordained by Mendes remained true to their new allegiance and suffered for their championship of the Roman Church. Among them was Abbot Orasi Krestos, who after a flogging and other brutal treatment was spreadeagled upon the ground in the market place, pegged down so that the people could trample on him and finally had his head smashed with a heavy stone.

The Portuguese settlers were permitted to remain. Their skills were used by the Emperor for the construction of his palace at Gondar, the site most probably chosen by Paez on the instructions of Susenyos. This was the first static capital of the country since Aksum, now reduced to a sprawling village after the Muslim invasions. While the court was itinerant both the Galla and domestic rebels had been held in check. As Gondar grew in splendour the boundaries of the Emperor's effective authority contracted. The rulers of the historic provinces became increasingly independent of the central government. Divergent views on the precise nature of Christ continued to be debated in the monastic schools. An attempt to reconcile differences under the Emperor David III led in 1721 to a proclamation from the gate of the palace of Gondar: the Word was 'perfect God and perfect man by the union of one Christ, whose body is composed of a precious substance called Baharî, not consubstantial with ours or derived from his mother'. There it rested incomprehensibly.

With the exclusion of foreigners the curtain came down once more on the empire of Prester John. Only with the accession in 1818 of Theodore II, whose long reign ended with suicide in 1868 after his defeat by a British force under Napier of Magdala, was an attempt made to reunify the country. Theodore's work was taken further by Menelik II who, after Gondar had suffered devastation in an earthquake, founded Addis Ababa and annexed the Muslim sultanates of Jimma and Harar. He recreated Ethiopia, the vast territory known to Paez, still imperfectly explored and still awaiting a peaceful development.

The achievement of the Jesuits, despite the ultimate débâcle of their mission, was nevertheless remarkable. Professor Edward Ullendorff considers it immense. He writes:

They helped a Christian nation to maintain its identity and independence against Muslim encroachment; they had notably contributed to the education of the people; and above all they had explored the country with remarkable diligence and truly astonishing courage and perseverance; and they have left us worthy records of their learning, monuments of scholarship far in advance of their time.

At the same time Ullendorf assesses the damage. Ascribing to the Jesuits as a body what was more properly the work of Mendes and those acting under his strict directions, he continues: 'By religious intolerance and narrow-mindedness they rendered nugatory all attempts at real advance; they implanted in the people a deep-seated suspicion of Europeans . . . and threw them back into an isolation which lasted for centuries.'

It is questionable whether the Jesuits, left to the methods advocated by Ignatius and pursued by Paez, would have met with ultimate success. What is unquestionable is their unselfish devotion to Ethiopia. 'I do not know any country in the world,' wrote Almeida, 'not even Portugal where I was born, for which I have a greater affection than this one.' The same could have been said to a man by the Spanish, Italian and Portuguese Jesuits who worked with him. James Bruce, with all his prejudices, sought like Paez to understand the Ethiopian mind. He rightly saw the expulsion of the Jesuits as a reassertion of the national religion, but his comparison with the Glorious Revolution of 1688 in England is less apposite. Perhaps the last word belongs to Sir Wallis Budge, who writes that 'had Paez lived a few years longer the history of Abyssinia from 1623 to 1632 would have been different'.

Appendix 1

Sources

This book draws mainly on the fifteen-volume work of C. Beccari entitled *Rerum Aethiopicarum Scriptores Occidentales*. Published between the years 1903 and 1917, it contains letters, journals, histories and reports on Ethiopia taken for the most part from the central Jesuit archives in Rome. The collection, which was subsidized by the Italian government, has been used surprisingly little by all writers on the country. The material is mostly in Portuguese, Spanish, Latin and Italian and spans the entire period of Jesuit activity there. Among these volumes I have drawn principally on Volume XI, *Relationes et Epistolae Variorum* (Pars Prima, Liber II), 1589-1623, and Volume XII, *Relationes etc.* (Pars I, Liber III), 1622-35. In these two volumes, which together amount to more than a thousand pages, can be found most of the letters to which I have referred. Volumes II and III comprise Paez's *Historia Aethiopiae*. As I have used this work a great deal I have noted in a separate appendix Paez's own sources, which make it possible to trace easily the authority for most of his statements.

Almeida's book with the same title (Volumes V, VI and VII) is based principally on Paez as far as the year 1622, but takes the story of the Jesuits in Ethiopia to the end of their mission there. Sections of Almeida's *History* have been translated into English and edited by Professor C. F. Beckingham and G. W. B. Huntingford in *Some Records of Ethiopia, 1593-1646*; this work contains a 'Gazetteer of Ethiopian Place Names' indispensable to the study of the country in this period.

Volume VIII in Beccari's series, Mendes's *Expeditio Aethiopica*, the only volume written in Latin, has been used in Chapter 8 of this book. I have referred only occasionally to the remaining seven volumes, which deal with years that lie outside the scope of this book. The discursive index to each volume of Beccari makes it easy to trace my sources in detail. The alternative would have been a multiplicity of footnotes which would have given the book an air of academic scholarship that it does not merit. Only occasionally have I placed a note at the bottom of a page with the purpose of illuminating the text.

The only manuscript material I have used consists of four unpublished letters of Paez. These are to be found in the Jesuit archives in Rome among the papers recovered from the Italian state, which confiscated them in 1870. Two of these letters have been used in Chapter 1: the first (Indipetae, Vol.26, no.84) is the request made by Paez to Acquaviva to be sent on the missions; the second, also written to Acquaviva, expresses Paez's readiness, after his return from captivity in Yemen, to set out again for Ethiopia (Goa-Malab., Epis. 14, f. 333). A third letter, dated 26 June 1611, is directed to Fr. A. Mascarenhas, the General's Assistant for Portuguese affairs; in it Paez explains why the time is not opportune to institute a search for the remains of Cristovão da Gama (Goa-Malab., Epis. 11, ff. 453-4).

The following list is not intended to present a bibliography of the Society of Jesus in Ethiopia but merely to indicate books and articles that I have found useful either generally or in detail.

Alphabeticum Aethiopicum sive Abyssinum cum oratione dominicali, etc. Typis Congregationis de Propaganda Fide (Rome, 1631).

Alvares, Francisco, *Narrative of the Portuguese Embassy to Abyssinia*, translated and edited by Lord Stanley of Alderley (Hakluyt Society, 1881).

Beckingham, C. F., 'Some Early Travels in Arabia' in *Journal of the Royal Asiatic Society of Great Britain and Ireland* (London, 1949).

Beckingham, C. F., 'Jeronimo Lobo: his travels and his book' in *Bulletin of John Rylands Library*, Vol. 64, no.1 (1981).

Beckingham, C. F. and Huntingford, G.W. B., *Some Records of Ethiopia, 1593-1646* (Hakluyt Society, 1954).

Beckingham, C.F. and Huntingford, G.W.B., *The Prester John of the Indies: the Portuguese Embassy to Ethiopia, 1520* (Cambridge, 1961)

Beke, C., *Memoire justificatif en réhabilitation des Pères P. Paez et J. Lobo en ce que concerne leurs visites à la source de l'Abbai (Le Nil)*, etc. (1848).

Brando, Mario, *Colegio das Artes* (Coimbra, 1942).

Bruce, James, *Travels to Discover the Source of the Nile*, five volumes (Edinburgh, 1768).

Bruce, James, *Travels, etc.*, selected and edited by C. F. Beckingham (Edinburgh, 1964).

Budge, Sir E. A. Wallis, *A History of Ethiopia*, Vol. 2 (London, 1936).

Casanovas, R. E. P., *Orazio Grassi e le Comete dall' anno 1618* (Vatican Observatory).

Cheesman, R. E., *Lake Tana and the Blue Nile* (London, 1936).

Cooley, M. W. Desborough, 'Notice sur le Père Pedro Paez' in *Bulletin de la Société de Géographie* (Paris, 1972).

Crawford, R. E., *Ethiopian Itineraries* (Hakluyt Society, 1958).

Frend, W. H. C., *The Rise of the Monophysite Movement* (Cambridge, 1972).

Grassi, Orazio, *De Tribus Cometis Anni MDCXVIII* (Rome, 1619).

Harden, J. M., *An Introduction to Ethiopic Christian Literature* (London, 1926).

Hoyland, J. S., *The Commentary of Father Monserrate on his Jouney to the Court of Akbar* (Oxford, 1922).

Jones, J., The Decision of the Holy Office on Abyssinian Orders' in *The Month*, no. 19 (1873), 451-60.

Jones, J., 'On Abyssinian Ordinations' in *The Month*, no. 20 (1874), 228-40.

Kammerer, M. A., 'Le plus Ancien Voyage d'un Occidental en Hadhramout' in *Bulletin de la Société Royale de Géographie de l'Egypte*, no. 18 (Paris, 1933), 143-67.

Kircher, Athanasius, *Mundus Subterraneus*, vol. 2 (Amsterdam, 1678).

Levine, Donald N., *Wax and Gold: Tradition and Innovation in Ethiopian Culture* (University of Chicago Press, 1974).

Lobo, Jerome, *A Voyage to Abyssinia*, translated by Dr Johnson, in J. Pinkerton, *Voyages and Travels*, Vol. 15 (London, 1814).

Lockhart, Donald M. and Da Costa, P. M. G., *The Itinerario of Jerónimo Lobo*, with an Introduction by C. F. Beckingham (Hakluyt Society, 1984).

Lubienietski, S., *Historia Universalis Omnium Commetarum* (1681).

Mendes, A., 'Oratio Habita Philippi III Hispanarum Regi, Lusitaniae II, in Academia Eborensi', in A. Vasconcelles, S.J., *Anacephaeoses* (1621), 589-96.

Mathew, David, *Ethiopia* (London, 1947).

Monumenta Historica Societatis Jesu: Monementa Ignatia, vol. 2 (Rome).

Moorhead, Alan, *The Blue Nile* (London 1962).

Pakenham, Thomas, *The Mountains of Rasselas: An Ethiopian Adventure* (London, 1959).

Pankhurst, Sylvia, *Ethiopia: A Cultural History* (London, 1955).

Poncet, J., *A Voyage to Ethiopia, 1698-1701* (Hakluyt Society, 1949).

Rey, C. F., *The Romance of the Portuguese in Abyssinia* (London, 1929).

Salt, H., *A Voyage to Abyssinia* (London, 1814).

Schurhammer, G., *St Francis Xavier*, Vol. 2, translated by M. J. Costelloe (Rome, 1977).

Sumner, Claude, *Ethiopian Philosophy*, vol. 3 (Addis Ababa, 1978).

Tacchi-Venture, P., 'Pietro Paez, Apostolo dell'Abissinia al Principio del Secolo XVII in *Civiltà Cattolica*, Vol. 3 (1905), 560-81.

Tellez, Balthazar, *The Travels of the Jesuits in Ethiopia* (London, 1710).

Tesiger, Wilfred, *Arabian Sands* (London, 1959).

Thurston, Herbert, 'The Eucharist in the Abyssinian Church' in *The Ecclesiastical Review*, no. 94 (1936) 227-38.

Thurston, Herbert, 'Abyssinian Devotion to Our Lady' in *The Dublin Review*, no. 198 (1936) 227-38.

Ullendorff, Edward, *The Ethiopians: An Introduction to the Country and the People*, (Oxford, 1965).

Varones Illustres de la Compagñia de Jesus: Misiones de la China, Ethiopia, Malabar, ed. 2, Vol. 2 (Bilbao, 1889).

Wessels, C., 'Pedro Paez, 1622-1922' in *Studies*, Vol. XCII (1922), 1-20.

Appendix 2

Paez's Authorities

Paez's *History of Ethiopia* was written in his last years in the country. Since I have relied a great deal on his work, it would perhaps be right to list his sources. He himself reduces them to three: Ethiopian books, the testimony of reliable witnesses, and his own observation. To these a fourth should be added: books, both published and unpublished, by Europeans, mainly Portuguese, who were cognizant of Ethiopia, a source that he himself frequently cites.

I *Ethiopian books*

1 The list of kingdoms and provinces of the Empire given to P. by the secretary of Susenyos.
2 Two lists of Emperors, the first found by P. among the books of the church of Aksum, the second given to him by Susenyos.
3 A book entitled, *Kebra Nagast* (*Glory of the Kings*), found by P. in the church of Aksum; from this P. drew the tradition of the Queen of Sheba and her son, Menelik.
4 *The Chronicle of Zara Jakob*, given to P. by Susenyos.
5 *Mazaquebt Haimanot* (*The Treasury of the Faith*).
6 *Haimanot Abau* (*The Faith of our Fathers*).
7 *Codex Ceremoniarum pro Coronatione Imperatorum*, which P. found among the books at Aksum.
8 *Liturgia Aethiopica*, which P. translated literally into Portuguese.
9 *Liber Precum in usum Monachorum*, which was given to P. by the Superior of a monastery.
10 *Ceremoniale*, which was used by the Abuna for conferring Orders, written in Arabic; the book was seen by P. who was not permitted to read it.
11 *Ritus et Preces in Initiatione Monachorum*, from which P. gives extracts.

163

12 *Vita Abba Stateus*. What P. wrote about Estateus he got from monks who possessed this book, but he himself never had it in his hands.

13 *Vita Abba Tackla Haimanot*. The whole book is given by P. in Portuguese.

14 *Vita Abba Samuel*, from which P. gives certain excerpts.

15 *Synaxarium*, which P. translated with the title *Flos Sanctorum*. The book has an appendix on the life of the Emperor Lalibela.

16 *Acta S. Frumentii*. This is P.'s authority for stating that in the Ethiopian books there is no mention of the sacraments of confirmation and extreme unction.

17 Ethiopian books to which he does not give a title. P. drew on them in part for the offices of the Ethiopian court.

II *Oral tradition gathered from reliable sources*

1 Leading courtiers: for the frontiers of the empire in the time of Susenyos; from an unnamed courtier for information about the first and last time the Emperor's sons were guarded on amba Guexen.

2 Za Oald Madehen, Superior of the monastery of Allelo: for the statement that the Dominicans were unknown in Ethiopia in recent times.

3 State officials: for the changes in public offices in Susenyos's time.

4 Three princes, descendants of ancient Emperors and living on the amba Guexen: for information about the amba and its inhabitants. Two of these princes: for the treasures of the amba.

5 The Abba Merca: for the way Emperors were chosen.

6 Gabriel, the Portuguese: for details of the coronation of Susenyos; for the electric fish in the river Nile.

7 An old monk learned in ritual: for the way the feast of the Holy Cross was celebrated in Ethiopia.

8 Persons knowledgeable in Ethiopian traditions: for the kind of women the Emperors married.

9 Za Dengel: for the statement that Ethiopians were unfamiliar with Portuguese laws.

10 Susenyos: for the way princes were guarded on the amba Guexen; the treasures there; for the election of Emperors; the method of hunting rhinoceros; the course of the Nile; the alleged equestrian Order; doubts on the validity of ordinations.

11 Cela Krestos: for the same.

12 Treasurer and Secretary of the Emperor: for taxes and tributes in the time of Susenyos.

13 A Portuguese in da Gama's expedition: for details of da Gama's death.

165

20 Principal monasteries.
21 Hallelujah monastery.

IV *Portuguese works*

1 Alvares, Francisco, *Verdadeira informaçao das terras do Preste
João das Indias* (Lisbon, 1540): for description of chairs or seats of
stone surrounding the old church at Aksum which did not exist in P's
time; for the dress the Emperor Onag Sagad wore; for the way the
Emperor marched; for the rock churches; the way of giving judgement.

2 Guerreimo, Ferdinand, *Relaçam com huma addiçam á relaçam
de Ethiopia nos annos 1608-1609*, (Lisbon, 1611): for the testimony
of the Patriarch Oviedo; *re* the Council of Trent; for the history of da
Gama; the reception of Oviedo by the Emperor Claudius.

3 Castanhoso, Miguel de, *Historia das cousas que Christóvão da Gama
fez nos reynos do Preste João* Lisbon, 1548): for da Gama.

4 Alvares, João, S. J., Assistant for Portugal: for letter about the
validity of Ethiopian Orders based on the testimony of Oviedo (11,
13, no.6).

Appendix 3

Note by Professor C. F. Beckingham on illustration facing page 84

The illustration facing page 84 is one painting. The manuscript (B.L.Or.713) from which it is taken is an account of the miracles of St George. The two figures on horseback are St George and St Mehnam. The story is this. A fisherman threw his net and caught a large number of fish in it. When he began to haul it in, it tore. He appealed to St Mehnam. He in turn appealed to St George; both were on horseback. St George replied that the man had not appealed to him, but to Mehnam. They both then plunged their lances into the water and retrieved the net. The fisherman realized the pre-eminence of St George and noticed that Mehnam had addressed him deferentially. The narrative which runs to about half a page, has been published in the *Corpus Scriptorum Christianorum Orientalium*, series aethiopica, tom. 31 (Ethiopic text), tom. 32 (Latin text).

Comparative Chronology

Emperors	Kings of Portugal	Popes	Abunas	Jesuit Activity
Minas (Admas Sagad) 1559-63	Sebastian 1557-78	Pius V 1566-72		Oviedo's Patriarchate 1556-77
Sarsa Dengel (Malak Sagad) 1563-97	Henry I 1578-80	Gregory XIII 1572-85	Mark 1567	
Jakob 1597-1604	Philip I (Philip II of Spain)	Sixtus V 1585-90		Paez's First Journey 1588-95
Za Dengel 1604	1581-98	Urban VII 1590	Christodulus	
Jakob (again) 1604-5		Gregory XIV 1590-91		
		Innocent IX 1591		
		Clement VIII 1592-1605	Peter (killed in battle 1605)	Paez's mission 1603-22
Susenyos (Seltan Sagad) 1605-32	Philip II (Philip III of Spain) 1598-1621	Leo XI 1605		
	Philip III (Philip IV of Spain) 1621-40	Paul V 1605-21	Simon (1605-17)	
		Gregory XV 1621-23		
				Mendes's Patriarchate 1625-33
		Urban VIII 1623-44	Rezek 1635	
Fasiladas (Alam Sagad) 1632-65			Mark 1636	

Index

Mocha, 38; a galley slave, 38; returns to Goa, 39; falls sick, 40; at Salsette, 40; sails from Diu (1603), 44; reaches Massawa, 44; and Fremona, 46; visits Hallelujah monastery, 47; waits for invitation to court, 48; meets Za Dengel, 49; preaches to court, 51, 52, 62; studies Ethiopian texts, 63, 82; translates Bellarmine, 66; understands Ethiopian ethos, 68; on Eucharist, 69; sails in tankua, 70; greeted by S, 71; suffers fever, 74; holds theological discussions, 74, 78; joins S in campaigns 75, 77; on Guexen, 75; at Dancaz, 79; tries to avert rebellion, 86; stops request for Patriarch, 88; on ordinations, 89-90; on clergy, 90; his gifts to S, 90; builds palace, 91-2; offers to go to Rome, 93; to Agau, 104; on source of Nile, 105-10; on its course, 110; on torpedo fish, 112; advises bleeding for Cela Krestos, 115; at congress of religion, 118; warned against poison, 117; advises against slavery, 125; builds church, 125-6; interprets comet, 127; writes his *History*, 129-31; death, 132; correspondence with Iturén, 19, 23, 31, 35, 37, 43-5, 107, 130-2; with Jeronimo Xavier, 1-2, 4, 93-5; his *History* cited, 46, 69, 70, 89, 107, 108, 131

Pankhurst, Professor Richard, viii, 59

Pate (island), 135

Paul II, 8

Paul III, 10

Paul V, 80, 93-4, 116-17, 131

Pereira, Bernardo, 135-6

Pereira, Simão de Mello, 117

Peter, Abuna, 54, 57, 139, 140

Philip I (Portugal), II (Spain), 25, 39, 40, 41

Philip II (Portugal), III (Spain), 42, 53, 80, 81, 94, 116-17, 134

Philip III (Portugal), IV (Spain), 137-8, 142, 147

Ptolemy, Philadelphus, 106

Piedro (Ethiopian), 10

Pius V, 15

Poncet, Jacques, 148n

Pounde, Thomas, 20

Propaganda, Congregation of, 147

Qanobin, 124

Qatna, 31

Qishn, 28, 133

Razuam Aga, 43-5

Rezeq (Rezek), Patriarch, 155

Ribadeneira, Pedro, 85

Ricci, Matteo, vii, 3-4, 41-2, 52, 123

Rocha, João, 138, 139, 142

Rodrigues, Antonio, 22

Rodrigues, Gonzalo, 11-13

Romano (Mangonio), Lorenzo, 56, 66, 120

Rudolph (lake), 100

Sahala, 105, 110

Salsette, 40, 41

Samuel, Abbot, 47

San'â, 33-7, 39, 93; Pasha of, 32, 35; his wife, 37

Santaren, Ferdinand, 19

Sarka, 98

Sarsa Dengel, Emperor, 14, 48, 52, 54, 58, 107, 152

Sarsa Krestos, 150, 152

Sebastian (King of Portugal), 15, 23, 127-8

Seco, Didaco (Bishop), 138